Gospel Sermons

by

Three Generations of Preachers

by

Father:
Johnie Edwards

Son:
Johnie Paul Edwards

Grandson:
John Isaac Edwards

Sermons Reflect 100 Years
of Study and Preaching

ISBN 10: 1-58427-3356

ISBN 13: 978-1-58427-3356

Guardian of Truth Foundation
CEI Bookstore
220 S. Marion St., Athens, AL 35611
1-855-49-BOOKS or 1-855-492-6657
www.truthbooks.net

Table of Contents

His Eye Is on the Sparrow

Introduction

1. Do you ever get to thinking that nobody cares?
2. God cares (1 Pet. 5:7).
3. Song: "His Eye Is on the Sparrow."

Discussion

I. His Eye Is on the Sparrow.

A. Psalm 84:3

B. Luke 12:6-7

C. Can you imagine how many sparrows there are in the world? God knows them all, even when one falls to the ground!

D. We are much more valuable than a sparrow.

II. God's Eyes.

A. The Bible says much about God's eyes:

1. They are filled with grace (Gen. 6:8; Eph. 2:8; Tit. 2:11; 1 Cor. 15:10).
2. They are in every place (Prov. 15:3; 2 Chron. 16:9; Ps. 139:7-8; Zech. 4:10).
3. They behold the evil and the good (Prov. 15:3; 5:21; Job 34:21; Jer. 32:19).
4. They are upon the righteous (Ps. 34:15; 1 Pet. 3:12; Job 36:7; Isa. 59:1-2).
5. They are upon His promises (Gen. 12:1-3; Deut. 11:10-12; Jer. 30:3; Josh. 21:45; 1 Kings 8:56; 2 Pet. 1:4; 3:9; Gal. 3:26-29). We sing, "I'm standing on the promises of God."

B. Don't ever forget the all-seeing eyes of God.

III. How God Has Shown That He Watches Us.

A. He is mindful of us (Heb. 2:6; Ps. 8:3-4; Acts 17:28).

B. He provides a way of escape from temptation (Heb. 4:15; Matt. 4:1-11; 1 Cor. 10:13; Jas. 1:12-15).

C. He has made salvation possible (Gen. 3:15; Gal. 3:16; 4:4; 1 Tim. 2:3-4; Isa. 45:22; Rom. 5:8; John 3:16; Rom. 8:3).
D. He planned and purposed the New Testament church (Eph. 3:10-11; Acts 2:47; Matt. 16:18; Acts 20:28).
E. He told us what to do to be saved (Acts 18:8; 2:38; Mark 16:16) and made heaven possible (John 14:1-6; 2 Cor. 5:1).

IV. The Song, "His Eye Is on the Sparrow."

A. Jesus is our friend (John 15:13-14).
B. Jesus said, "Let not your heart be troubled" (John 14:1).
C. "Resting on His goodness" (Acts 10:38; 1 Pet. 2:21-22).
D. "Whenever I am tempted," Jesus can say, "I was also tempted" (Heb. 4:15; 2:17-18).
E. "From care he sets me free" (Song: "Does Jesus Care?").
F. "I sing because I'm happy, I sing because I'm free" (Song: "Sing and Be Happy").

Conclusion

1. You can't say that nobody cares, for "His eye is on the sparrow, and I know He watches me.
2. This is the right place and the right time, so come as we stand to sing.

How to Treat One Another

Introduction

1. The New Testament uses the phrase "one another" some 34 times.
2. Many churches are filled with contention, fussing, and fighting.
3. We must learn to get along if the work of the church is to progress.

Discussion

I. Edify One Another.

- A. Romans 14:19; Ephesians 4:29
- B. The word "edify" means to build up or strengthen.
- C. I need to always measure what I say and do by how it might affect others.
- D. Instead of focusing on our problems, we should focus on ways we can encourage each other.
- E. We can edify one another by:
  1. Worshipping together (Col. 3:16).
  2. Teaching (Acts 20:32).
  3. Showing appreciation (1 Tim. 2:1).

II. Be Kind One to Another.

- A. Ephesians 4:32; Galatians 5:22; 1 Corinthians 13:4
- B. Some Christians display a cold, sour disposition.
- C. Kindness begins with the smile. "You're never fully dressed without a smile!"
- D. Kindness means never being rude or mean. It leads us to do thoughtful things for others.

III. Use Hospitality One to Another.

- A. 1 Peter 4:9
- B. Hospitality literally means "the love of strangers." It involves giving a warm and friendly welcome.
- C. It is important for a church to be friendly to visitors.
- D. It is equally important that brethren show hospitality to one another "with-

out grudging."

E. Hospitality helps to promote love and unity, integrate new members, encourage weak members, etc.

IV. Prefer One Another.

A. Romans 12:10; Philippians 2:3

B. Most people prefer themselves. They put their own wants, opinions, and feelings first. Pride and selfishness are contrary to the spirit of humility.

C. Some have a "my way or else" spirit. It is the same spirit of Diotrephes, "who loveth to have the preeminence" (3 John 9).

D. We must work together!

V. Forgive One Another.

A. Ephesians 4:32; Mark 11:26; Colossians 3:13

B. We often make mistakes and need forgiveness. Therefore, we should be understanding and forgive others.

C. We cannot hold grudges, bitterness, hatred, malice, etc. within our heart.

D. "Forgiveness is the fragrance given off by the violet when crushed."

VI. Love One Another.

A. John 13:34-35; 1 John 4:11

B. Too many churches split asunder with fussing and fighting.

C. We must learn that we can disagree without being disagreeable!

D. Treat others with love and respect.

Conclusion

1. All of these will promote unity.
2. We need the spirit of the song, "He ain't heavy, he's my brother!"

Going to the Ant

Introduction

1. Solomon said, "Go to the ant, thou sluggard; consider her ways, and be wise" (Prov. 6:6).
2. Let's go to the ant and consider her ways. It should not be difficult to go to the ant as ants are found almost everywhere and at any one time there are at least 1 quadrillion living ants on the Earth.

Discussion

I. Consider Their Division of Labor.

A. In an ant colony that may number upward of 20 million ants, you'll find a queen or queens, the female worker ants, and the males.

B. In some species in which the ants vary in size, subcastes are distinguishable. That is, you find certain members carrying out specific functions with some tending the larvae and others foraging for food.

C. While *all* Christians have work to do, there is a sort of division of labor in the Lord's church (Eph. 4:11-12). But, this body of believers is "fitly joined together" and "maketh increase of the body" (Eph. 4:16).

1. Elders who oversee (1 Pet. 5:2).
2. Deacons who serve (1 Tim. 3:8-12).
3. Evangelists who preach (2 Tim. 4:2).
4. Members one of another who depend upon each other (1 Cor. 12:12-27) and by love serve one another (Gal. 5:13).

D. The song "Room in God's Kingdom" expresses it well when it says, ". . . There is room, there's a place, There is work that we all can do."

II. Consider Their Foresight.

A. We see their foresight or care in providing for the future in that they provide their food in the summer and gather their food in the harvest (Prov. 6:8).

B. Evidently ants are good planners.

C. Each ant must have some foresight for he has "no guide, overseer, or ruler" but still instinctively prepares by adding to the common store.
D. The sluggard is advised to consider the ants foresight and wake up or come to poverty (Prov. 6:9-11).
E. God's people need foresight in planning for the future:
   1. Parents need it (Eph. 6:4).
   2. Christians need it (2 Pet. 2:18).
   3. Churches need it (Eph. 4:16).
F. "Where there is no vision a people perish" (Ralph Waldo Emerson).

III. Consider Their Unwearied Activity.

A. "Provideth her meat in the summer, and gathereth her food in the harvest" (Prov. 6:8) – they store their provisions in the summer and gather their food at harvest.
B. The ant is careful to make preparation through unwearied activity so as to be prepared when needed.
C. "The ants are a people not strong, yet they prepare their meat in the summer" (Prov. 30:25).
D. The context of both occurrences (Prov. 6:8; 30:25) suggests the harvester ant that lives in arid environments and depends almost totally on seeds.
E. The work and activity of God's people needs to be like that of an ant, unwearied and undaunted (John 9:4; 2 Cor. 12:15; Gal. 6:9; 2 Thess. 3:13; 1 Cor. 15:58).
F. We need the mind of Nehemiah and his workers who did so much in just 52 days (Neh 4:6).

Conclusion

1. If the ant prepares for her future, how much more should we be preparing for our future as we must give account of ourselves to God (Rom. 14:12).
2. We would do well to prepare to meet God (Amos 4:12).

What A Blind Man Saw

Introduction

1. Acts 9:1-9
2. While blind, Saul saw some things that we need to see.

Discussion

I. Conscience Is Not a Safe Guide in Religion.

A. In religion, many let their conscience be their guide.

B. Conscience tells us whether we are doing right or wrong, based upon what we have been taught.

C. Saul was guided by his conscience (Acts 23:1), but did many things which were wrong (Acts 26:9).

D. Personal feelings can lead one astray (Prov. 14:12).

II. Being a Religious Person Is Not Enough.

A. Some think that as long as you're a religious person that is enough in pleasing God.

B. Saul of Tarsus was a very religious individual (Gal. 1:13; Acts 26:5).

C. Saul was even zealous in his religion (Gal. 1:14).

D. He saw that he was religiously wrong.

III. One Can Transgress by Following Traditions.

A. Many just follow the traditions handed down to them.

B. Saul followed the traditions of his fathers (Gal. 1:14).

C. The Lord taught that one transgresses the commandment of God by following the traditions of men (Matt. 15:1-6).

D. The only traditions that we can follow are those handed down by the apostles (2 Thess. 2:15; 3:6).

IV. The Need for the Right Source of Authority.

A. There are two sources of authority in religion: Heaven and men (Matt. 21:23-27).

B. Saul received authority for the things he did from men (Acts 9:14; 26:10).

C. Christ is the source of authority to which we must always go (Matt. 28:18; Col. 3:17).

V. Man Is Not Saved By Prayer Alone.

A. Some believe that to be saved they must just pray.

B. Saul prayed to God (Acts 9:11).

C. If Saul was saved by prayer, he was saved before he was told what he had to do to be saved (Acts 9:6).

VI. What One Must Do to Have His Sins Forgiven.

A. Some never do see what they must do to have their sins forgiven.

B. Acts 9:6

C. To have his sins washed away, Saul had to be baptized (Acts 22:16).

VII. Salvation Is an Individual Affair.

A. Acts 9:6

B. The Philippian Jailor asked, "Sirs, what must I do to be saved?" (Acts 16:30).

C. We must save ourselves (Acts 2:40; Phil. 2:12).

VIII. The Chiefest of Sinners Can Be Saved.

A. Some think that they have committed such sins that they can never be forgiven.

B. 1 Timothy 1:13-16

C. If Saul was saved, then no matter what you have done, you can be saved!

D. The gospel is for all (Rom. 1:16; Mark 16:15-16).

Conclusion

1. Saul of Tarsus saw these things while blind.
2. Can you see these things?

Some Things We Must Not Forget

Introduction

1. There are many things which we must not forget that have been written in the Bible (1 Tim. 4:6; 2 Tim. 1:6; 2:14; 2 Pet. 3:1).
2. I would like to call to your attention some of these:

Discussion

I. We Must Not Forget the Lord.
   A. Deuteronomy 6:12
   B. Deuteronomy 8:11, 14, 19
   C. Jeremiah 2:32
   D. Psalm 19:7

II. We Must Not Forget the Benefits of the Lord.
   A. Psalm 103:2
   B. James 1:17
   C. How would you like to do without God's sunshine, air, and rain?

III. We Must Not Forget the Word of the Lord.
   A. Psalm 119:16, 83, 109, 141, 153, 176; Acts 20:35
   B. To guard against forgetting the Word of God, we must study (2 Tim. 2:15).

IV. We Must Not Foret the Poor Among Us.
   A. Psalm 74:19
   B. Galatians 2:10; Matthew 26:11; 25:34

V. We Must Not Forget the Works of God.
   A. Psalm 78:7
   B. Psalm 19:1

VI. We Must Not Forget Our Creator in Our Youth.

A. Ecclesiastes 12:1
B. Many reasons for remembering the Creator in youth:
   1. Less to repent of.
   2. Bad habits have a way of getting hold on people.
   3. Less to reap (Gal. 6:7).
   4. Before evil things become pleasure and frailties of old age set in.
   5. For a proper example (1 Tim. 4:12).
   6. The young die too!

VII. We Must Not Forget That Life Is Short.

A. Psalm 89:47
B. Just how short is life?
   1. Few days (Job 14:1).
   2. As grass (1 Pet. 1:24; Ps. 103:15).
   3. A step (1 Sam. 20:3).
   4. A moment (2 Cor. 4:17).
   5. As a tale told (Psa. 90:9).
   6. Swifter than a weaver's shuttle (Job 7:6).
   7. As a shepherd's tent (Isa. 38:12).
   8. Young, but now old (Ps. 37:25).

VIII. We Must Not Forget Those in Bonds and Adversity.

A. Hebrews 13:3 — Many Christians in the days of this writing were in prison and adversity.
B. Some continue today in adversity.

IX. We Must Not Forget the Lord's Death.

A. 1 Corinthians 11:23-26
B. This is one purpose for the Lord's Supper.
C. To be remembered every week (Acts 20:7).

X. We Must Not Forget Lot's Wife.

A. Luke 17:32
B. We must not look back (Luke 9:62).
C. If we go back, notice the condition (2 Pet. 2:20-22).

XI. We Must Not Forget Jesus Christ.

A. 2 Timothy 2:8
B. He will return (John 14:3).
C. That He died (1 Cor. 15:1-6).
D. Psalm 9:17

XII. We Must Not Forget the Consequences of Sin.

A. Romans 6:23 — Death
B. James 1:14-15

C. Revelation 20:12-15 — Spiritual death

Conclusion

1. While there are some things we must not forget, there are some things that we must forget:
   a. The wrong others do us (Eph. 4:31-32).
   b. Those things which are behind (Phil. 3:13-14).
2. How's your memory?

"God Was Not Well Pleased"

Introduction

1. We can learn from the mistakes of others.
2. The Old Testament was written for our admonition and learning (1 Cor. 10:11).
3. Text: 1 Corinthians 10:1-11
4. The Israelites sinned, God was not pleased with them, and they were punished. The same thing can happen to us!
5. Let us consider the five specific sins committed by the Israelites (1 Cor. 10:6-10) in three parts:
   a. When Israel committed the sin.
   b. How this might have applied to Corinth.
   c. How this applies to us today.

Discussion

I. **"Lust After Evil Things."**
   A. Israel lusted wandering in the wilderness (Num. 11:4-6, 33-34).
   B. The Corinthians were struggling with lust – after meats, idolatry, immorality.
   C. Many struggle with lust today.
   D. 1 Timothy 6:9; Galatians 5:16-17; Romans 13:14
   E. Temptation stems from within, with our own lusts (Jas. 1:14). We must have the strength to say no.
   F. Keep your heart and thoughts pure.

II. **"Neither Be Ye Idolaters."**
   A. Israel made and worshipped the golden calf (Exod. 32:1, 4-6).
   B. The Corinthians faced the problem of idolatry by joining in the pagan festivities, eating meats sacrificed to idols, etc. (1 Cor. 10:14, 20-21).
   C. We can be guilty of the same thing if we worship anything but God.
   D. Idolatry would also include giving the devotion which belongs to God to something else. One can make an idol out of money, pleasure, sports, TV,

etc. (Eph. 5:5; Matt. 4:10).

III. "Neither Let Us Commit Fornication."

A. Israel committed fornication (Num. 25:1-2, 9).

B. In Corinth was the temple of Aphrodite, where 1,000 prostitutes were kept. Part of their idol worship involved sex with these women (1 Cor. 6:9-11).

C. Today fornication is a major problem.

D. By age 19, nearly 80% of young people have had sex outside of marriage.

E. Sex is honorable and a blessing in marriage (Heb. 13:4).

IV. "Neither Let Us Tempt Christ."

A. Israel did (Num. 21:4-6).

B. The Corinthians were trying God's patience by wanting to sin.

C. Many today try to tempt Christ by:

1. Placing themselves in temptation.
2. Complaining and rebelling.
3. Weakness and a lack of faith.

D. Matthew 4:7

V. "Neither Murmur Ye."

A. Israel constantly complained (Num. 11:1; 14:1-11).

B. The Corinthians were complaining over Paul's (Christ's) restrictions.

C. Many grumble and complain today.

D. Complaining indicates a lack of faith, and selfishness. It spreads unhappiness and discouragement.

E. "I would rather light one small candle than to curse the darkness."

Conclusion

1. Results: God not pleased; overthrown (1 Cor. 11:5).
2. It can happen to us too!

The Role of Children in the Family

Introduction

1. The role of children in the family is determined by God's Word and not by time and circumstances.
2. The role of children in the family is:

Discussion

I. To Honor Their Father and Mother.

A. Exodus 20:12; Deuteronomy 5:16; Matthew 15:4; 19:19; Mark 10:19; Ephesians 6:2-3
B. This is showing "piety at home" (1 Tim. 5:4) and it's the "first" responsibility of every child!
C. To honor means to give the proper esteem.
D. Children honor their parents by being obedient to them (Eph. 6:1).
E. Honor so that it "may be well with thee. . ." (Eph. 6:3).
F. Children can properly honor their parents as they show "piety at home" (1 Tim. 5:4).

II. To Hear a Parent's Instruction.

A. Proverbs 1:8-9
B. Proverbs 4:1-4, 10-22; 6:20-25; 23:22
C. To listen to a father's instruction is a means of gaining wisdom (Prov. 13:1).
D. By the time a child reaches the age of accountability he knows beyond much doubt what his father would say in almost every situation that arises whether the father is present or not.
E. Young people who think they have a monopoly on wisdom are headed for trouble. Remember Rehoboam?

III. To Obey Their Parents.

A. Ephesians 6:1-3
B. "Obey" – "to hear under (as a subordinate), i.e. to listen attentively; by impl. to heed or conform to a command or authority:—hearken, be obedient to, obey" (Strongs).
C. Colossians 3:20
D. It is easy for a child who is old enough to have ideas of his own to obey his parents when they suggest the things that he wants to do. It is an entirely different matter when they suggest things that are contrary to his desires. *That is when the true spirit of obedience can be seen!*
E. Children should obey willingly and pleasantly and a child who does otherwise is a rebellious child!
F. If parents require something of a child that is a violation of the will of God, then "we ought to obey God rather than men" (Acts 5:29; Matt. 10:37).

IV. To Cleanse Their Way.

A. Psalm 119:9
B. Cleansing one's way or making one's life what it ought to be is something to be done by all!
C. Children, as they are growing toward maturity, will sin and transgress God's law (Rom. 3:23; 1 John 3:4).
D. At an early age, we must come to appreciate the terrible consequences of sin in our lives (Rom. 6:23).
E. Sin can be cleansed (Acts 2:38; 3:19; 8:22). Baptism cleanses the past sins of the alien sinner (Rom. 3:25). Repentance, confession, and prayer cleanse the sin of the child of God (James 5:16).
F. Sin and wrongdoing must be cleansed! It cannot be forgotten, set aside as not important, or ignored!
G. 1 Timothy 4:12; 2 Timothy 2:22

V. To Remember Their Creator in the Days of Their Youth.

A. Ecclesiastes 12:1
B. Solomon counseled youth to remember God while young, before the dark days of old age (Eccl. 12:1-7).
C. Young people should see youth as a time to serve God with many opportunities.
D. As a youth, Daniel, along with his friends, purposed in his heart to do the will of the Creator (Dan. 1:8).
E. Youth is not a time for rebellion against God, parents, and civil authority! It is the time to remember God!

VI. To Bear the Yoke.

A. Lamentations 3:27
B. The idea of bearing a yoke is the idea of working and accepting responsibility.

C. A yoke was a wooden frame placed on the backs of draft animals to make them work in tandem.
D. The yoke is necessary for youth and it is good for youth as it conquers self-will and the idle love of pleasure and trains in self-denial.
E. Resistance to the yoke's of life is wrong and foolish. Submission is right and wise!

VII. To Be Sober Minded.

A. Titus 2:4-6
B. To be sober minded is to be of sound mind and self-controlled.
C. Sobermindedness would include being free from the harmful effect of intoxicants like alcohol, illegal drugs, and nicotine as they harm the body and mind and don't glorify God (1 Cor. 6:19-20).
D. Sobermindness includes being in control of one's thoughts, desires, passions, and lusts. It is having the right mind and attitude (Phil. 4:8).
E. Surely this would include having a grateful mind.

Conclusion

1. Such children maketh a glad father (Prov. 10:1), give "delight unto thy soul" (Prov. 29:17), and will not be "the heaviness" of their mother (Prov. 10:1).
2. "Even a child is known by his doings, whether his work be pure, and whether it be right" (Prov 20:11).

Golden Lessons from a Golden Calf

Introduction

1. While Moses was upon mount Sinai, Israel made a golden calf and worshipped it (Exod. 32:1-6).
2. Let's notice some golden lessons from this golden calf.

Discussion

I. The Importance of Patience.

A. The Israelites lacked patience.

1. Moses assured the people that he would return (Exod. 24:14-18).
2. Israel "saw that Moses delayed to come" and made themselves gods (Exod. 32:1).

B. A lack of patience caused Israel to turn aside from obeying God (Exod. 32:8).

C. As Israel was to be patient for the coming of Moses, we must be patient for the coming of the Lord (2 Thess. 3:5).

II. Sin Is Observed by An All-Seeing God.

A. God saw the sin of Israel (Exod. 32:7-9).

B. Some try to hide their sins from God (Gen. 3:8).

C. God sees all that we do (Prov. 5:21; Heb. 4:13).

D. The Psalmist knew that he could not escape the all-seeing eye of God (Ps. 139:7-12).

E. The secrets of men will be made known at the judgment (Rom. 2:16).

III. Sin Has Penalty.

A. Sin does not go unpunished!

B. Sin brought the wrath of God and about three thousand men died (Exod. 32:9-10, 28).

C. The penalty for sin is spiritual death (Rom. 6:23).

IV. Idolatry Is a Great Sin.

A. When Israel made the golden calf and worshipped it, they "sinned a great sin" (Exod. 32:30).
B. Sin is the transgression of God's law (1 John 3:4).
C. The Law of Moses forbade idolatry (Exod. 20:3-5).
D. We are guilty of idolatry when we commit covetousness (Col. 3:5).
E. We must "flee from idolatry" (1 Cor. 10:14).

V. Atonement Must Be Made For Sin.

A. Moses sought to make atonement for the sin of Israel (Exod. 32:30-35).
B. On the day of atonement, the high priest went into the most holy of holies and offered an atonement sacrifice (Lev. 23:27-28; Heb. 10).
C. We receive atonement for sin through Christ (Rom. 5:11) by being baptized into His death (Rom. 6:3-4).

VI. God Blots Sinners Out of His Book.

A. Exodus 32:30-33
B. God has a book in which the faithful are enrolled.
   1. Philippians 4:3
   2. Revelation 3:5
   3. Revelation 20:12
   4. Revelation 20:15
   5. Revelation 21:27
C. Your name can be blotted out of the book!
D. Is your name written there?

Conclusion

1. May we learn these golden lessons from the golden calf.
2. Make atonement for your sins now so that your name can be added to God's book!

Things of Christ

Introduction

1. The Bible identifies a number of things that are "of Christ" (Phil. 2:21).
2. It's good for us to know the things of Christ.

Discussion

I. Churches of Christ.

A. Romans 16:16

B. The church is identified as belonging to Christ.

C. The church belongs to Christ because:

1. He built it (Matt. 16:18).
2. He is its head (Col. 1:18).
3. He shed His blood for it (Acts 20:28).

D. Acts 2:47 and Ephesians 5:23 show the importance of the Lord's church.

II. Blood of Christ.

A. Matthew 26:28; Ephesians 1:7; Romans 5:9; 1 Peter 1:8-10; Revelation 1:5

B. The blood saves when we are baptized into the death of Christ (John 19:34; Rom. 6:3-4).

III. Gospel of Christ.

A. Romans 1:16-17; 1 Corinthians 15:1-6; Mark 16:15-16; Ephesians 1:13; Colossians 1:5

B. The word "gospel" means "the good news," the good news about Christ.

C. The gospel is God's power to save us from our sins when we obey it (2 Thess. 1:7-9).

IV. The Lord's Supper.

A. Communion (1 Cor. 10:16; Matt. 26:26-28).

B. 1 Corinthians 11:20, 23-34

C. To be taken on the first day of the week (Acts 20:7).

V. Day of the Lord.

A. Revelation 1:10; Psalm 118:24
B. Philippians 1:10

VI. Cross of Christ.

A. 1 Corinthians 1:17; Galatians 6:12; Philippians 3:18
B. Jesus died on the cross for man (Heb. 2:9; John 19).

VII. Words of Christ.

A. Colossians 3:16
B. John 12:48

VIII. Love of Christ.

A. Romans 8:35
B. 2 Corinthians 5:14

IX. Work of Christ.

A. Philippians 2:25-30
B. 1 Corinthians 15:58; John 9:4

X. Doctrine of Christ.

A. 2 John 9-11
B. Doctrines means teaching.

XI. Mind of Christ.

A. 1 Corinthians 2:16
B. Philippians 2:5-8
C. Romans 8:9

XII. Judgment Seat of Christ.

A. 2 Corinthians 5:10
B. All will appear before this seat!

Conclusion

1. Are you ready to appear before the judgment seat of Christ and give account?
2. You can make ready right now!

"These Things Doth The Lord Hate"

Introduction

1. Proverbs 6:16-19
2. This is a numerical proverb, or a *midda*.
3. All seven things are hated by the Lord.

Discussion

I. "A Proud Look."

- A. Literally, it means "haughty eyes."
- B. Some people's lofty expression reveals the swelling pride within.
    1. They think they are better than everyone else - look down on others.
    2. They become cocky and arrogant.
- C. Proverbs 16:5
- D. We are to be humble and meek (Matt. 5:5).
- E. We must dispense with our pride.

II. "A Lying Tongue."

- A. Psalm 119:163
- B. We hate to be called "liars," but we don't mind lying!
- C. At first it might appear that lying is the best way to go.
    1. It might get you out of trouble.
    2. It might save you some money.
    3. It might make you look better.
- D. But in every case you lose far more than what you may momentarily gain — that is your integrity!
- E. "Honesty is the best policy!"

III. "Hands That Shed Innocent Blood."

- A. This refers to the murderer.
- B. God hates the taking of human life.

1. Cain cursed for killing Abel (Gen. 4).
2. God gave Noah a law against murder (Gen. 9:6), for we are "in his image."
3. Exodus 20:13; Revelation 21:8

C. Violence and murder have become common – drive by shootings, Oklahoma bombing.
D. Life is precious, to be cherished.

IV. "An Heart That Deviseth Wicked Imaginations."

A. Here is a heart that is scheming, plotting, planning wicked things. It has become the devil's workshop.
B. We must keep the mind pure (Prov. 4:23; 23:7; Phil. 4:8).
C. An imagination is a wonderful blessing, but it can become a curse, if we fantasize ourselves doing evil.

V. "Feet that Be Swift in Running to Mischief."

A. Here is one eager to get involved in sin.
B. 1 Thessalonians 5:22; Ephesians 5:11; 1 Corinthians 6:9-11
C. Learn to say "No!" and make it stick.

VI. "A False Witness That Speaketh Lies."

A. Exodus 20:16
B. Many a person has perjured himself to screen the guilty, or ruin the innocent.
C. Another application here may involve gossip. Much of it involves untruths.
D. Before you repeat a story, ask yourself: Is it true? Is it fair? Is it necessary? If not, then shut up!

VII. "He That Soweth Discord Among Brethren."

A. If "Blessed are the peacemakers" – Then "Cursed are the troublemakers!"
B Psalm 133:1; Galatians 5:15
C. Many churches have those who are contentious, always stirring up trouble.
D. Peace is prompted by love and respect.

Conclusion

Revelation 21:27

Discipline in the Family

Introduction

1. "And ye fathers, do not provoke your children to anger; but bring them up in the discipline and instruction of the Lord" (Eph. 6:4, NASV).
2. The Hebrew writer taught that discipline or chastisement yields the "peaceful fruit of righteousness" (Heb. 12:5-11, NASV).
3. We focus our attention on the discipline of children in the family.

Discussion

I. What Is Discipline?

A. Basically, discipline is training! It is training that is expected to produce a specific character or behavior.

B. Discipline can be of two types:

1. *Instructive Discipline.* This discipline is preventive in nature. This is what we do in all of our teaching and encouragement.
2. *Corrective Discipline.* This discipline is penalizing in its nature. It corrects, punishes, or chastises.

C. Discipline should not be confused with abuse!

1. Discipline is discipline and abuse is abuse! Discipline suggests the proper training, while abuse suggests ill or improper treatment.
2. Proper discipline will bring about the peaceable fruit of righteousness, while abuse will bring discouragement and wrath (Col. 3:21; Eph. 6:4).

II. The Value of Discipline.

A. Discipline or chastisement yields the "peaceful fruit of righteousness" (Heb. 12:5-11, NASV).

B. Discipline is essential as it is the training that trains "up a child in the way he should go: and when he is old, he will not depart from it" (Prov. 22:6).

C. The results of discipline include respect (Heb. 12:9), wisdom (Prov 29:15), and rest (Prov 29:17).

III. Discipline and the Scriptures.

A. A number of Bible scriptures speak concerning discipline.

B. A number of passages in Proverbs speak concerning discipline (Prov. 3:11-12; 12:1; 13:24; 15:5, 10, 32; 19:18; 22:6, 13-15; 29:15, 17).

C. Jeremiah 2:30

D. Ephesians 6:4

E. Parents would do well to heed the words of God!

IV. Eli and His Undisciplined Sons.

A. Eli's sons were serving as priests and had corrupted the priesthood (1 Sam. 2:12-17).

B. The corruption of Eli's sons was not limited to disrespect for God's orders concerning sacrifice, but was also prevalent in their moral conduct. Their immorality was common knowledge, and the report of it eventually reached their father (1 Sam. 2:22-25).

C. The prophet came forth to announce God's judgment against the wickedness of Eli's sons (1 Sam. 2:27-34).

D. When the Lord called Samuel, He revealed His tragic prophecy concerning Eli (1 Sam. 3:10-14).

E. Hophni and Phinehas were cut off in one day (1 Sam. 4:10-11).

F. It's disturbing to see how Eli neglected his sons. Their service was a mockery because they did not know the Lord (1 Sam. 2:12-17).

G. Eli's message for us today is for us to give our family the attention they deserve and need.

Conclusion

As we instruct and train our children, let's be sure that we are bringing them up in the discipline and admonition of the Lord!

"He Careth For You"

Introduction

1. Do you ever feel as if no one cares?
2. The Psalmist felt that way (Ps. 142:4).
3. The Scriptures teach that Jesus cares (1 Pet. 5:7; Matt. 9:36; Matt. 23:37; Mark 4:38-39).
4. Here are things Jesus has done which show that He cares.

Discussion

I. Jesus Became Poor That You May Be Rich.
  A. 2 Corinthians 8:9
  B. Jesus took the form of a servant (Phil. 2:5-7).
  C. He did this so that you can lay up treasures in Heaven (Matt. 6:19-20).

II. Jesus Became Homeless That You May Have a Home.
  A. Matthew 8:20
  B. The Lord has gone to prepare a mansion for you in Heaven (John 14:1-3).
  C. This will be an eternal home (2 Cor. 5:1-6).

III. Jesus Became Hungry That You May Be Fed.
  A. Jesus fasted and was hungry (Matt. 4:2).
  B. You can be fed with living bread (John 6:51, 57-58).
  C. Matthew 4:4

IV. Jesus Became Thirty That You May Drink.
  A. Jesus thirsted (John 4:7; 19:28).
  B. You can drink of the water of life (John 4:10-14).
  C. You are invited to drink of the living water (Rev. 22:17).
  D. Those who hunger and thirst after righteousness will be filled (Matt. 5:6).

V. Jesus Became Weary That You May Have Rest.
  A. Jesus was wearied (John 4:6).
  B. Jesus has promised rest (Matt. 11:28-30).

C. We must labor to enter the rest (Heb. 4:9, 11).

VI. Jesus Wept That You May Have Your Tears Wiped Away.

A. Jesus wept (John 11:35; Luke 19:41).

B. God will wipe away all tears from our eyes when the former things are passed away (Rev. 21:4).

C. This shows that Jesus cares!

VII. Jesus Was Made a Curse That You May Be Blessed.

A. Galatians 3:13-14

B. You can enjoy blessings in Christ (Eph. 1:3).

C. Baptism puts one in a place of blessings (Gal. 3:27).

VIII. Jesus Died That You May Live.

A. Jesus died for every man (Heb. 2:9).

B. Jesus died for sinners (Rom. 5:8).

C. Since Jesus died, you can live forever (Rom. 5:9-10; 1 Thess. 5:10).

IX. Jesus Shed His Blood That You May Be Redeemed.

A. Jesus shed His blood on the cross (John 19:34).

B. We have redemption through His blood!

1. Galatians 4:4-5
2. Ephesians 1:7
3. 1 Peter 1:18-19
4. 1 Corinthians 6:20

C. This blood is contacted in baptism (Rom. 6:3-4).

Conclusion

1. Truly, Jesus cares for you!
2. Do you care enough for Him to obey Him now?

Sabbath Keeping

Introduction

1. Confusion exists as to which day is to be kept as a day of worship. Only the Bible can settle the issue.
2. The issue is not, was the Sabbath ever binding, but is it binding on men today?

Discussion

I. Sabbath Belonged to the Jewish Age.

- A. No command or example for Sabbath keeping until a "test run" (Exod. 16:4, 22-26).
- B. The Law of Moses:
    1. Sabbath command and penalty (Exod. 20:8).
    2. Sabbath given to Israel after Egyptian bondage (Exod. 20:1-2, 8).
    3. Sabbath reminded Israel that they had been slaves in Egypt (Deut. 5:15).
    4. Sabbath was a sign between God and Israel (Exod. 31:12-17; Ezek. 20:10-12).
    5. Sabbath given at Sinai (Neh. 9:13-14).

II. No Distinction in Law of Moses and Law of God.

- A. Sabbatarians say that the law of God and the law of Moses are two different laws.
- B. These two laws are the same (2 Chron. 34:14; Ezra 7:6; Mark 7:10; 2 Chron. 31:3; Neh. 8:1, 14; Luke 2:22-24).

III. Ten Commandments Done Away in Christ.

- A. 1 Kings 8:9, 21; Exodus 34:28
- B. Deuteronomy 4:13; 9:9-11
- C. Jeremiah 31:31-34; Hebrews 8:7-13
- D. Christians dead to the law (Rom. 7:1-7).
- E. Sabbath law nailed to the cross (Col. 2:14-17).
- F. Live under New Testament (2 Cor. 3:6-14; Gal. 6:2).

IV. Sabbath Keepers Do Not Keep the Sabbath Law.

A. Sabbatarians fail to obey laws regulating the Sabbath.
B. The Sabbath:
   1. A rest day (Exod. 35:1-3; 20:8-10).
   2. Violation penalty (Num. 15:32-36).
   3. Burnt offering required (Num. 28:9-10).
   4. Travel restricted (Acts 1:12; Exod. 16:29).
C. Sabbath keepers are not consistent!

V. The First Day of the Week.

A. God chose the first day of the week as the day of worship.
B. This was the day:
   1. Christ arose from the dead (Mark 16:9; Luke 24:1).
   2. Jesus met with His disciples (John 20:1, 19, 26).
   3. The great events of Acts 2 happened (Lev. 23:15; Acts 2).
      a. First gospel sermon preached.
      b. Many obeyed the gospel.
      c. The Lord's church began.
   4. The church assembled (1 Cor. 11:18-20; Acts 20:7; 1 Cor. 16:1-2).

Conclusion

1. The Sabbath day served its purpose and God took it out of the way (Gal. 4:21-31).
2. Today, the first day of the week is the day of worship.

Giving God Our Leftovers

Introduction

1. Isaiah's sermon on idolatry (Isa. 44) shows that God is not content with the leftovers of a man's life.
2. Whenever our service unto God becomes merely an afterthought, it is unacceptable.
3. Yet many try to serve God this way, and end up with a religion of "leftovers."
4. Let's consider some areas in which people try to give God their leftovers.

Discussion

I. Loyalty.

A. God must come first (Matt. 6:33; 22:36-38).

B. Most people place God far down on their list of priorities. They have deeper loyalties to job, TV, sports, etc.

C. If God is not first in our life, then He will not be in our life – He won't take second place!

D. We must be totally committed to serving God.

II. Time.

A. Time is, "the stuff life is made of" (Benjamin Franklin).

B. It is our second most precious possession, second only to our soul.

C. It is precious because it means opportunities.

D. Ephesians 5:15-16; Psalm 90:12

E. We are busy. We spend time working, eating, sleeping, etc. If we are not careful all of these urgent pursuits cause us to put off the important things.

F. We should take the time for worship, study, prayer, teaching, good works, being with our families, and many other things of great importance.

G. These don't take much time, but they are productive of an eternity!

III. Money.

A. You work hard for a living.

1. You have to provide shelter. Probably, you have a mortgage to pay.

2. We have groceries to buy.
3. Clothing to purchase, medical expenses, etc.

B. If we are not careful, we spend all our money and have little left for God.

C. God's portion should come first, off the top, not off the bottom – leftovers.

D. 1 Corinthians 16:2; 2 Corinthians 9:7; Malachi 3:8-10

E. In Mark 12:41-44, who are we like: the poor widow who gave sacrificially, or the rich who gave "of their abundance"?

IV. Energy and Ability.

A. Most of us exhaust our energy and use our abilities in our work, or in some hobby.

B. It is easy to expend all our talent and energy in these areas and then have little left for God.

C. In the Parable of the Talents (Matt. 25), Jesus teaches us to use our talents for the Lord.

D. Luke 12:48; 1 Corinthians 15:58; Titus 2:14

E. Let us strive to, "Be, all that you can be," in the Lord's army.

V. Life.

A. Many people have the idea that religion is for old folks, those who are worried about dying.

B. Some want to live their life for themselves, enjoying the world, then at the last moment, turn to the Lord.

C. Ecclesiastes 12:1; Romans 12:1; 1 Corinthians 6:19-20

D. Colossians 3:3-4 – Is Christ your life?

Conclusion

1. God deserves, demands, and expects more than the crumbs that fall from life's table.
2. He expects our best, not leftovers!

"There Is A Generation"

Introduction

1. Text: Ecclesiastes 1:4
2. Many generations have come and gone over time and they can differ greatly.
3. Let's notice "there is a generation."

Discussion

I. "There is a generation that curseth their father, and doth not bless their mother."

A. Proverbs 30:11
B. Such is a sad generation!
C. The fifth commandment (Exod. 20:12).
D. Punishment was death (Exod. 21:17; Deut. 21:18-21).
E. Proverbs 23:22
F. Ephesians 6:1-3

II. "There is a generation that are pure in their own eyes, and yet is not washed from their filthiness."

A. Proverbs 30:12; 16:2
B. Remember the self-righteous Pharisee of Luke 18:11?
C. Proverbs 16:25; Jeremiah 10:23
D. Sometimes a generation will come along that has the idea that they can do whatever they want and it's okay.
E. James 1:21
F. Ephesians 5:1-5
G. Romans 1:22
H. We need to repent of our sins (Acts 3:19) and be washed from the filthiness of sin (1 Cor. 6:9-11).

III. "There is a generation, O how lofty are their eyes! and their eyelids are lifted up."

A. Proverbs 30:13

B. This refers to an arrogant generation.
C. Proverbs 16:18; 29:23
D. 1 John 2:16
E. Among the things that the Lord hates is a proud look (Prov. 6:16), pride, and arrogance (Prov. 8:13).
F. God resists the proud (Jas. 4:6).
G. Our generation needs humility (Rom. 12:3, 10, 16).

IV. "There is a generation, whose teeth are as swords, and their jaw teeth as knives, to devour the poor from off the earth, and the needy from among men."

A. Proverbs 30:14
B. "But ye have despised the poor. . ." (Jas. 2:6) as some have had little concern for others, especially the poor.
C. Our Lord was poor and taught responsibility to such (Matt. 25:42).
D. Matthew 19:21
E. Zacchaeus promised to give half his goods to the poor in restitution for his wrong (Luke 19:8).
F. Acts 20:35
G. Ephesians 4:28
H. When God's love dwells in us then we will have a heart of compassion (1 John 3:17-19).

V. There is a "chosen generation."

A. 1 Peter 2:9
B. This "chosen generation" was the "elect" of God (1 Pet. 1:2), had purified their souls in obeying the truth (1 Pet. 1:22), and had a "lively hope. . ." (1 Pet. 1:3-4).
C. This is a spiritual generation or race (NAS)!
D. This spiritual generation or race is "the people of God" who have obtained mercy (1 Pet. 2:10).
E. As God's "chosen generation," we should be showing forth His praises (1 Pet. 2:9) or "excellencies" (NAS).
F. Are you a part of this "chosen generation"? Those who have purified their souls in obeying the truth?

Conclusion

What kind of generation will we prove to be?

Giving Glory unto God

Introduction

1. Psalm 29:1-2, 9
2. We are to give God the glory that is due unto Him.
   a. Romans 15:6
   b. 1 Corinthians 10:31
3. Here are some ways we can give glory unto God.

Discussion

I. Give Thanks unto God.

A. Luke 17:11-19
B. A leper gave glory unto God by giving thanks!
C. Many today are unthankful (2 Tim. 3:1-2; Rom. 1:21).
D. We have so much to be thankful for!
   1. The victory in Jesus (1 Cor. 15:57).
   2. The obedience of others (Rom. 6:17).
   3. Our brethren (2 Thess. 2:13).
   4. All things (Eph. 5:20).
E. Have you given thanks unto God, lately?

II. Sing Praises unto God.

A. Romans 15:9
B. Psalm 50:23
C. Psalm 69:30
D. Hebrews 2:12
E. Singing is a means of teaching and admonishing one another (Eph. 5:19; Col. 3:16).
F. A mechanical instrument in worship does not give glory unto God!

III. Properly Honor and Use the Physical Body.

A. 1 Corinthians 6:18-20
B. We must be good stewards of the body which God has given unto us!

C. We properly use the physical body by presenting our bodies a living sacrifice (Rom. 12:1-2).
D. We must keep our bodies pure (1 Tim. 5:22).

IV. Bear Much Fruit unto God.

A. John 15:8
B. We bear fruit by keeping the commandments of Christ (John 15:1-10).
C. We should bring forth fruit unto God (Rom. 7:4).
D. How fruitful are you?

V. Pray to God in the Name of Jesus.

A. John 14:13-14
B. Prayer is how we communicate with God (Phil. 4:6).
C. We pray to God in the name of Jesus (John 15:16; Col. 3:17).
D. Jesus Christ is the mediator between God and men (1 Tim. 2:5).
E. How long has it been since you prayed to God?

VI. Confess Jesus as the Son of God.

A. Philippians 2:9-11
B. A centurion glorified God when he confessed Jesus as the Son of God (Matt. 27:54; Luke 23:47).
C. The Lord demands that we confess Him before men (Matt. 10:32-33).
D. Confession is made unto salvation (Rom. 10:9-10).
E. The eunuch confessed Jesus (Acts 8:37).
F. Have you confessed your faith in the Son of God?

Conclusion

Have you given glory unto God?

Clay in the Potter's Hand

Introduction

1. The word "made" is found 1311 times in the Bible. It sometimes refers to the fact that "in the beginning, God made" all things (Gen. 1:7, 16, 25, 31; 2:2-4, 9, 22; 3:1). It means to create or bring into being.
    a. Hebrews 11:3
    b. Colossians 1:16-17
2. The Potter and the clay (Isa. 64:8).
    a. "Clay" used 30 times.
    b. "Potter" used 8 times.
    c. Jeremiah 18:1-6
    d. Romans 9:21
3. Song: "Clay in the Potter's Hand."

Discussion

I. God Made Man.

A. Genesis 1:26-27
B. Genesis 2:7
C. Psalm 100:3
D. Ecclesiastes 7:29
E. James 3:9
F. Psalm 139:14

II. God Made Man Male and Female.

A. Homosexuals are often heard to say, "We were just made that way!"
    1. Genesis 1:27
    2. 1 Corinthians 11:8-9
    3. Genesis 2:18-24
B. Both the Old and New Testaments condemn homosexual activity.
    1. Leviticus 18:22
    2. Leviticus 20:13

3. Romans 1:26-32
4. 1 Corinthians 6:9
5. 1 Timothy 1:9-11
6. 2 Peter 2:6-7
7. Jude 7

C. Abuse of the body carries penalty.
   1. Romans 1:27
   2. HIV virus brings about "Acquired Immune Deficiency Syndrome" known as "aids."
   3. Sickness and disease are known among those who practice this shameful sin.

D. Hebrews 13:4; 1 Corinthians 7:2-5

E. We are told the potter made this clay that way, with these desires. Not so! None of the animal kingdom engage in such homosexual activity! God created the woman for the man, to be a helper "meet" (suitable) for him and joined them together in a beautiful relationship called marriage.

III. What the Potter Has Made of Some in the Past.

A. The Ephesians (Eph. 2:11-16).
   1. Note how he molded them (Acts 19:1-6).
   2. Their obedience changed their lives.

B. The Corinthinans (1 Cor. 6:9-11).
   1. How did God mold them?
   2. Acts 18:8
   3. They were called saints (1 Cor. 1:1-2).

C. The Jews who crucified Christ (Acts 2:1-47).
   1. Acts 2:22-23
   2. How did God accomplish this? (Acts 2:36-41, 47)

D. Saul of Tarsus
   1. Acts 7:58
   2. Acts 8:1-3
   3. Galatians 1:13
   4. 1 Timothy 1:13-15
   5. How did God change this man? (Acts 9; 22:16; 26)

IV. What God Has Made Us

A. We are His workmanship.
   1. Ephesians 2:8-10
   2. Created for good works as individuals (Matt. 5:14-16; Phil. 2:15; Tit. 3:1; 1 Tim. 5:10).
   3. Let God through His Word mold you into a good works person!

B. Kings and Priests.
   1. Revelation 1:6

2. Revelation 5:10
3. We have a special relationship with God. We as priests can talk with Him through His Son.
4. We are royalty as Kings (1 Pet. 2:5-10).

C. Free.
1. Galatians 5:1
2. Galatians 5:13; 1 Peter 2:16
3. How does God make us free? (Rom. 6:17-18, 1-6; Gal. 3:26-27).

D. Accepted.
1. Ephesians 1:6
2. How? (Eph. 1:7).

E. To sit together in heavenly places.
1. Ephesians 2:6
2. How did He do this? (Eph. 2:1-10)

F. Meet to be partakers of the inheritance of the saints.
1. Colossians 1:12
2. Imagine God can mold us into such fashion that we can inherit His blessings (Matt. 25:34; 1 Pet. 1:3-4; Rom. 8:16-18; 2 Cor. 4:16; 5:1-6).

Conclusion

1. You can become a "new creature" in Christ (2 Cor. 5:17).
2. This is the right time and place to be baptized into Christ (Gal. 3:27).

Zacchaeus "Sought To See Jesus"

Introduction

1. Luke 19:1-10
2. The story of Zacchaeus is one we normally learn in children's Bible class.
3. But there is much more to the story, than a short man climbing into a tree.
4. It is the story of triumph, as Zacchaeus overcame many hindrances to see Jesus.
5. Many fail to find Jesus for these reasons.

Discussion

I. Riches.

A. Zacchaeus was rich (Luke 19:2).
B. Jesus had just finished teaching how difficult it is for a rich man to go to Heaven (Luke 18).
C. 1 Timothy 6:10, 17
D. Zacchaeus was a rich man who knew he was in need – in need of a Saviour!
E. Many today fail to find Jesus because of money. More worship the almighty dollar than God Almighty.

II. Position.

A. He was "chief among the publicans" (Luke 19:2).
B. A publican was a tax collector, working for the Roman government.
C. This would have made Zacchaeus a very important man. He was somebody!
D. But he was not as concerned about who he was as who Jesus was!
E. People's position keeps them away from the Lord.
   1. 1 Corinthians 1:26
   2. "In my position I can't afford to be a member of the church of Christ!"

3. As you move up, don't "outgrow" Jesus!

III. The Crowd.

A. Zacchaeus could not see Jesus for the crowd.
B. He was short and in a big crowd and would have had trouble seeing.
C. He overcame this problem by running ahead and climbing into a sycamore tree.
D. Notice that he was not as concerned with what others thought of him as he was with seeing Jesus.
E. Many times the crowd holds us back. Out of fear of being laughed at, we compromise and go along.
F. Romans 12:1-2; John 12:42-43

IV. His Past.

A. Zacchaeus seems to be promising restitution (Luke 19:8).
B. This is a sign of a changed heart.
C. He shows sorrow and penitence.
D. Many do not find Jesus because of sin in their past!
E. It matters not what you have been, Jesus is there for the finding!
F. "There is no saint without a past, and no sinner without a future!"
G. Philippians 3:13-14; Acts 13:39

V. Challenges.

A. Zacchaeus had every reason to give up and quit, but he found a way! Against all odds, overcoming all obstacles, he diligently sought Jesus and found Him!
B. Many quit seeking Jesus because of challenges: family, financial, sin, failure, fatigue, church problems, etc.
C. God's blessings are greater than any challenge.
D. James 1:2-4; 2 Peter 1:6

Conclusion

1. Zacchaeus found Jesus and responded (Luke 19:6, 9).
2. We, as well, can triumph over all hindrances with the same kind of diligence.

Going for the Gold

Introduction

1. As you watch the Olympics, you're impressed with going for the gold.
2. As Christians, we're going for the gold! We're striving for Heaven and it is described in the book of Revelation as a city of gold (Rev. 21:8, 21).
3. What is necessary for the child of God in winning the gold?

Discussion

I. Desire.

A. The athletes of the Olympic games have a strong desire and they are going for the gold.
B. Our burning and consuming desire must be Heaven! One can only go to Heaven when he has a strong desire to go!
C. Philippians 1:23
D. Hebrews 11:16
E. We should *"desire* the sincere milk of the word. . ." (1 Pet. 2:2).
F. This desire called "hope" is described as "an anchor of the soul, both sure and stedfast. . ." (Heb. 6:19).

II. Commitment.

A. Commitment is essential to the athletes of the Olympic games.
B. Our commitment to God and our Lord Jesus Christ must be real (Luke 10:27).
C. We pledge our obedience to Jesus Christ when we become the servants of God (Rom. 6:16-18).
D. 2 Timothy 1:12
E. This commitment was seen in the early Christians (Acts 2:42, 46; 4:32; 8:4).
F. We've just got to be committed! Nothing else will substitute for it!

III. Involvement.

A. The athletes of the Olympic games are involved.

B. As God's children, we must be involved as we go for the gold!
C. We sing, "There is much to do, there is work on every hand; Jesus calls for reapers, I must active be, What wilt Thou, O Master? Here am I, send me." Also, "Oh, the things we may do, you and I, you and I; Oh, the love we can give if we try; Just a word or a song as we're passing along, They will count in the great by and by."
D. Some were so involved that ". . . for the work of Christ . . . was nigh unto death. . ." (Phil. 2:30).
E. 1 Thessalonians 1:3
F. As we go for the gold, we must get involved and stay involved!

IV. Sacrifice.

A. Athletes of the Olympic games know what sacrifice is.
B. As we go for the gold, we have to make sacrifice.
C. Philippians 2:17
D. Romans 12:1
E. Hebrews 13:15
F.. We must deny ourselves of many things, as we go for the gold (Luke 9:23).

V. Endurance.

A. Athletes of the Olympics know about endurance.
B. As Christians, we must endure to the end (Jas. 5:11).
C. 2 Timothy 2:3
D. Mark 13:13
E. James 5:7-8
F. Hebrews 12:1-2

Conclusion

1. As we go for the gold, may we strive diligently so as to be able to hear these words (Matt. 25:21).
2. 1 Corinthians 9:25

Lessons from Moses and the Rock

Introduction

1. Numbers 20:1-13
2. Many good lessons can be learned from the story of Moses and the rock of Meribah (Rom. 15:4).

Discussion

I. God's Law May Change.

A. In Rephidim, Moses was told to smite the rock and water would come forth (Exod. 17:1-7)

B. In Kadesh, Moses was told to speak to the rock and water would come forth (Num. 20:7-8).

C. God's law for receiving water from the rock changed.

D. There has been a change between the Old Testament and the New Testament (Heb. 7:12).

E. What God required under the Law of Moses, is not acceptable today.

II. Substitution for God's Way Is Rebellion.

A. Moses substituted smiting for speaking.

B. This may have seemed like a small thing, but it brought severe consequences.

C. Moses rebelled against God (Num. 20:24; 27:12-14).

D. We must respect God's ways (Isa. 55:8-9; Prov. 14:12).

III. The End Does Not Justify the Means.

A. Numbers 20:10-11

B. Moses got results, but that did not justify the wrong.

C. Although a thing might bring good results, that does not mean that it necessarily pleases God.

IV. A Failure To Glorify God Is Sin.

A. Moses failed to give God the glory for the water that came from the rock (Num. 20:10; Deut. 32:48-52).
B. We need to learn to give God the glory in our lives.
C. Humility is needed in serving the Lord (1 Pet. 5:5-6).

V. God's Law Is Strict.

A. Moses died for his transgression (Deut. 32:48-52).
B. The wages of sin is spiritual death (Rom. 6:23).
C. To avoid this death our sins must be forgiven by God.

VI. The Importance of Speech.

A. Moses spake "unadvisedly with his lips" (Ps. 106:33).
B. Our speech is important (Col. 4:6).
C. We must refrain the tongue lest we sin against God with our lips (1 Pet. 3:10; Jas. 1:26).

VII. Disobedience Keeps Us from the Promised Land.

A. The disobedience of Moses kept him from entering the promised land (Deut. 32:48-52).
B. The promised land of the Old Testament foreshadows Heaven, the home of the soul.
C. We must obey in order to enter (Heb. 5:8-9).

VIII. Leaders of God's People Can Go Astray.

A. Moses was the leader of God's people (Exod. 3:11).
B. Moses was the lawgiver (John 1:17).
C. God's leaders are not above sin.
D. Elders can err and be in need of a good rebuking (1 Tim. 5:19-20).

Conclusion

1. May we learn from the mistakes of Moses.
2. Christ, the rock of ages, was smitten that you might drink of the water of life (Isa. 53:4-5; John 4:14; 1 Cor. 10:4).
3. Come, drink of the water of life.

"By Means of Death"

Introduction

1. Text: Hebrews 9:15
2. A number of things are so and made possible by the death of Christ.

Discussion

I. There Is Redemption.

A. Hebrews 9:15

B. The blood of Christ flowed both ways from the cross. The blood flowed backward to forgive the sins of faithful Jews under the law and flows forward to forgive the sins of those who obey the gospel (Heb. 2:9).

C. Ephesians 1:7 and Romans 3:24 show that redemption is in Christ.

D. Galatians 3:27 tells us how to get into Christ.

II. We Have the Last Will and Testament of Christ.

A. Hebrews 9:16-17

B. It took the death of Christ to put the New Testament into force.

III. We Can Be Holy.

A. 2 Timothy 1:10.

B. There is no way man could be holy without the death of Jesus (Tit. 2:11-12).

IV. Men Can Be Reconciled to God.

A. Romans 5:10

B. Ephesians 2:15-16

C. There can be peace between Jews and Gentiles.

V. Delivered unto Victory.

A. Everyone wants to win. By the death of Christ we can be victorious.

B. 2 Corinthians 1:9-10

C. Romans 7:24

D. 1 Corinthians 15:54-58

VI. Resurrection of the Dead.

A. 1 Corinthians 15:21
B. Romans 6:9
C. Acts 2:24
D. Adam brought death, but Christ brought life!

VII. By Death Comes Life.

A. One must die in order to live.
B. 1 Corinthians 15:35-38

Conclusion

1. We must die in order to be saved (Rom. 6:1-8).
2. Romans 6:17-18
3. Obey now!

Why We Lose Our Young People

Introduction

1. Many parents are brokenhearted over the loss of their children – those lost from the service of the Lord.
2. Many churches lose about half of their young people.
3. Let's consider some possible reasons.

Discussion

I. Lack of Proper Teaching.

A. Faith is not inherited. It comes from learning God's Word (Rom. 10:17).

B. The church and the home should be teaching (Prov. 22:6; Eph. 6:4).

C. Let us make sure our children are properly taught to love God, how to worship, the plan of salvation, the value of obeying God, etc.

II. Hypocritical Parents.

A. You may be able to fool others, but not your kids! They know if you are the same person on Tuesday you profess to be on Sunday.

B. When they see a difference between practice and profession, they soon lose respect for their parents, and the religion they profess.

C. They quit the church with, "at least I'm not a hypocrite!"

D. Matthew 18:6; 23:25-28

III. Worldly Friends.

A. Many a good kid heads into trouble by running with the wrong crowd.

B. 1 Corinthians 15:33; Proverbs 24:1

C. Promote family togetherness, and your home as a gathering place. Let kids know there is guilt by association.

IV. Evil Influences.

A. We are surrounded by temptation in movies, TV, magazines, schools, etc.

B. Some good kids are influenced by these and led astray.
C. 1 Thessalonians 5:22; Ephesians 5:11; Proverbs 23:7
D. Some parents may contribute by not disciplining and allowing their kids to do whatever they want.
E. But don't go overboard and be unrealistic in shielding kids (Lam. 3:27).

V. Church Problems.

A. Many churches are filled with fussing.
B. Most of the time it involves petty things: personalities, opinions, power struggles, cantankerousness, etc.
C. We run many a preacher out, kept good men from wanting the eldership, and turned off many of our young people because of this spirit!
D. Galatians 5:15; John 13:34-35
E. Let's get along and work together in love as an example for our kids.

VI. That Is Their Choice.

A. Our children, like us, are free moral agents. They have the right to choose how they will live.
B. 2 Corinthians 8:12; Galatians 6:5; Romans 14:12
C. Our example, teaching, and influence can help lead, but they must choose.
D. It could be they grow up and choose not to believe in Jesus, or choose to live in sin.

Conclusion

1. Spend time with your kids, love them, teach them, show them. It is never wasted time!
2. Pray they will choose to serve the Lord!

God's Attitude Toward Hypocrisy

Introduction

1. To learn God's attitude toward hypocrisy we study the story of Ananias and Sapphira.
2. Text: Acts 5:1-11

Discussion

I. 5:1.

A. Read background from Acts 4:32.
B. Luke had spoken of the liberality of the early church. He gave them a good example of liberality, Barnabas.
C. Now he gives an example of how not to practice liberality, Ananias and Sapphira – a quite striking case of insincerity, hypocrisy, and of the just judgment of God on those who are guilty of such.
D. A man may not suffer immediately as did Ananias and Sapphira, but God will repay all their due!

II. 5:2.

A. Ananias kept part of the price "for himself" (NAS).
B. They secretly kept back part of the price for themselves, *while professing* to be giving all.
C. Sapphira had full knowledge of the action. Thus, Sapphira entered into the sin with Ananias.
D. ". . . Laid it at the apostles' feet" – this is what Barnabas had done earlier.

III. 5:3.

A. Peter knew Ananias' heart.
B. ". . . Satan filled thine heart" – is language for "planted the thought in your mind."
C. The "why" implies that resistance to the temptation had been possible, but they had allowed the temptation to take root and grow (Jas. 1:14-15).

D. ". . . to lie to the Holy Ghost" – to lie here equals to attempt to deceive. They had lied or attempted to deceive God! You can't deceive God!
E. The deception involved keeping back part of the price of the land, and yet pretending to be giving it all.
F. Here we see what hypocrisy is! It is "play acting." Hypocrisy assumes the appearance of being religious.

IV. 5:4.

A. Ananias had no excuse for his sin!
B. The land was his and he could do with it as he wished.
C. ". . .why hast thou conceived this thing in thine heart?" – Ananias had conceived the thing in his heart!
D. ". . .thou hast not lied unto men, but unto God" – through his actions he had become guilty of lying or attempting to deceive God.
E. All sin may not be against man, but all sin is against God (Gen. 39:9).

V. 5:5.

A. Ananias' death was not a natural occurance.
B. His death was an act of God. Peter even prophesies the death in the case of Sapphira.
C. What if God, today, would strike dead all the hypocrites in the church?
D. Fear came upon the church as a result of God's discipline.

VI. 5:6.

A. Poor men had their garments wrapped tightly about their bodies and rich men were wrapped in linen.
B. Ananias is immediately taken out and buried without notifying the next of kin.

VII. 5:7.

A. Three hours elapsed and Sapphira, Ananias' wife, comes in not knowing what had happened.
B. She did not know that her husband had been caught in hypocrisy and had been taken out dead.

VIII. 5:8.

A. Peter's question gave her an opening for repentance.
B. Sapphira made her own choice to lie!
C. A godly woman would have warned her husband about the deception and possibly saved him.
D. Her hypocrisy is clearly seen and comes from her own tongue and fixed her fate.

IX. 5:9.

A. With her failure to repent, confess her wrong, and persist in sin, Peter predicts judgment upon her.

B. "... agreed together to tempt the Spirit of the Lord?" – They had conspired to deceive the Spirit.

C. Now, for the very first time, Sapphira learns what had happened to her husband.

D. The burial party was at the door!

E. She was no less guilty in the sin than her husband and the same punishment should come upon her.

X. 5:10.

A. Her death was clearly an act of God.

B. Ever wonder what the burial party must have thought? Can you imagine what they must have thought when they returned to find another body?

C. They conspired together and were buried together.

XI. 5:11.

A. "And great fear" – Our conduct is likely to be much better when we realize that God sees, hears, and knows all that goes on (Eccl. 12:13-14).

B. Fear came upon the church and upon others. This accomplished its intended purpose, namely, causing men to have respect for the church and God's will.

Conclusion

Hypocrisy is a sin that will cause one to lose his soul. If guilty, we must repent and turn in obedience to God.

The People Before the Water Gate

Introduction

1. This study is a close look at the people before the water gate as recorded in Nehemiah eight.
2. May we have the desire to follow their example.

Discussion

I. They Gathered Themselves Together.

A. Nehemiah 8:1
B. They left their cities and villages and assembled to hear the Word of God.
C. We must not forsake the assembling (Heb. 10:25).

II. They Were United.

A. Nehemiah 8:1
B. There is a real need for God's people to be as one man.
C. Unity was the prayer of Jesus (John 17:20-23).
D. We must endeavor to keep unity (Eph. 4:3-6).

III. They Asked for the Word of God.

A. Nehemiah 8:1
B. No other book is as needed as the book of God.
C. The Bible is final and complete (2 Tim. 3:16-17; 2 Pet. 1:3).

IV. They Were Attentive.

A. Nehemiah 8:3
B. We need to listen to God's Word! They were attentive from the morning until midday.
C. How attentive are you?

V. They Made Provisions for Preaching.

A. Nehemiah 8:4

B. They built a pulpit of wood for the purpose.
C. Have you made provisions for preaching?

VI. They Stood Up.

A. Nehemiah 8:5
B. They stood out of respect for the Word of God.
C. Should we show any less respect for the Bible?

VII. They Were in Agreement with the Word.

A. Nehemiah 8:6
B. The word "Amen" means "I agree," "so be it."
C. We need to be in agreement with God's Word.

VIII. They Worshipped God.

A. Nehemiah 8:6
B. God is the object of our worship (Matt. 4:10).
C. We must worship in spirit and truth (John 4:24).

IX. They Stood in Their Place.

A. Nehemiah 8:7
B. They were in place so they would not disturb others.
C. We need to stand in our place (Judg. 7:21).

X. They Were Touched by the Word.

A. Nehemiah 8:9
B. The Jews were "pricked in their heart" (Acts 2:37).
C. Have you ever shed a tear in reading God's Word?

XI. They Were Happy.

A. Nehemiah 8:12
B. They were happy because they understood the Word.
C. We need to rejoice (Phil. 4:4).

XII. They Were Obedient.

A. Nehemiah 8:14-18
B. They listened with the desire to obey.
C. We must hear and do (Jas. 1:22-25).

Conclusion

1. What is your attitude toward God's Word?
2. Obey now while you have the opportunity.

First Century Attitudes Needed Today

Introduction

1. Attitude is important (Prov. 4:23; 23:7). Attitude is how we look at and feel about a thing.
2. Let's look at first century attitudes needed today.

Discussion

I. "But First Gave Their Own Own Selves to the Lord."

A. 2 Corinthians 8:5

B. It is difficult to get golks to really and truly give themselves to the Lord.

C. 1 Corinthians 6:19-20

II. "Spend and Be Spent."

A. 2 Corinthians 12:15

B. Ever wear yourself out in the Lord's service?

III. "Searched the Scriptures Daily."

A. Acts 17:11

B. 2 Timothy 2:15

C. This is the only way we will know the truth and then our faith will not have to stand in the wisdom of men (1 Cor. 2:5).

IV. "Received the Word as the Word of God."

A. 1 Thessalonians 2:13

B. If we could get folks to have this attitude toward the Word of God, we would have greater success in getting them to obey the gospel.

C. Acts 2:41

V. "I Am Clean."

A. Acts 20:27

B. Please note what made Paul clean.

C. He was interested in others and taught them the Word of God.

VI. "I Am Not Ashamed of the Gospel."

A. Romans 1:16-17

B. Some seem to be ashamed of the saving gospel. We need to realize that the gospel is the "gospel of our salvation" (Eph. 1:13).

C. The gospel contains God's righteousness (Ps. 119:172) which has the power to save.

VII. "Forgetting Those Things Which Are Behind."

A. Philippians 3:13-14

B. We can't live in the past and must not look back (Luke 9:62).

VIII. "I Can Do All Things Through Christ."

A. Philippians 4:13

B. Few have learned the secret of doing things!

IX. "Not Seeking to Please Men."

A. Galatians 1:10

B. A lesson preachers need to learn.

X. "I Am Ready."

A. Romans 1:15

B. 2 Timothy 4:6-8

Conclusion

1. These are all first century attitudes that are needed in the twentieth century and beyond.
2. What's your attitude about obeying the gospel of Christ?

Adding to Your Faith

Introduction

1. 2 Peter 1:5-11
2. We are to give diligence to add these things to our life. That means we have to work at it! The result is to secure your calling and election.

Discussion

I. Faith.

A. This is the foundation of Christianity (Heb. 11:6).
B. Faith comes by hearing God's Word (Rom. 10:17).
C. Faith should grow (2 Thess. 1:3).
D. Faith is more than believing certain facts. It is trust; firm persuasion that leads to a life commitment to serve the Lord (2 Cor. 5:7).

II. Virtue.

A. This term carries the idea of the moral strength and courage to do what is right.
B. 2 Timothy 1:7-8; Revelation 21:8
C. We should never be ashamed of Christ or the truth, but always stand up for them (Rom. 1:16).

III. Knowledge.

A. Knowledge of God's will is essential to spiritual growth and strength.
B. 1 Peter 2:2; 2 Peter 3:18; Hosea 4:6
C. Growing Christians will come to Bible class and will study their Bible daily.

IV. Temperance.

A. This is self control – discipline.
B. James 1:12-14; Proverbs 16:32
C. In our society of instant gratification, it is hard to get people to deny themselves and say no.
D. Paul likened the Christian to an athlete (1 Cor. 9:25-27), who has to be

disciplined to succeed.

E. It takes self control to say "no" to the evil and "yes" to the good.

V. Patience.

A. This is steadfastness, endurance, perseverance – the ability to hang in there and never give up.

B. There are many discouragements, without this quality we would never make it.

C. James 1:2-4; Hebrews 12:1; Matthew 10:22

D. "Every cloud has a silver lining." Adversity can make us *better* or *bitter* depending on our reaction.

VI. Godliness.

A. In a world of godlessness, we need more righteous living – godliness.

B. 2 Peter 3:11; 1 Timothy 4:8

C. The ship can be in the ocean, but you can't let it in the ship! The Christian must live in the world, but cannot allow the world to live in him!

VII. Brotherly Kindness.

A. Our relationship with our fellow Christians is an important part of growing.

B. 1 Peter 1:22; 1 John 5:1; Ephesians 4:32

VIII. Charity.

A. Charity is love – goodwill to others.

B. We are to love God, neighbor, spouse, children, enemies, etc.

C. Colossians 3:14; 1 Corinthians 13:1-8

Conclusion

The end result of adding these things to your life is that you will never fall and can go to Heaven (1 Pet. 1:10-11).

Lessons from the Baptism of Jesus

Introduction

1. Text: Matthew 3:13
2. Valuable lessons can be learned from the accounts (Matt. 3:13-17; Mark 1:9-11; Luke 3:21-22).

Discussion

I. Jesus Was Baptized.

A. He came to John intending to be baptized of him (Mark 1:9).

B. We would do well, not only to intend to be baptized, but to be baptized (Mark 16:16).

C. John preached the baptism of repentance for the remission of sins (Mark 1:4). Of course, the baptism of Jesus was an exception to this rule for He "knew no sin" (2 Cor. 5:21).

II. Jesus Was Baptized to Fulfill All Righteousness.

A. Matthew 3:15

B. "Jesus came not only to fulfill all the requirements of the law, but also all that wider range of righteousness of which the law was only a part" (McGarvey).

C. Though John's baptism was no part of the Mosaic law, it was, nevertheless, a precept of God (John 1:33).

D. We too must "fulfill all righteousness" by being baptized into Christ for the remission of our sins (Mark 16:16). When we're baptized, we obey the commands of our Lord and fulfill the requirements of righteousness.

III. When Jesus Was Baptized, He Was Immersed.

A. He was baptized of John in the Jordan.

B. Jesus was immersed or plunged into the Jordan River.

C. ". . . went up straightway out of the water. . ." (Matt. 3:16).

D. "... straightway coming up out of the water ..." (Mark 1:10).
E. The baptism of Jesus involved an immersion in water. Our baptism into Christ, the one baptism that Paul spoke of in Ephesians 4:4, involves an immersion in water (Acts 8:36-39).
F. Paul taught that baptism is a planting "together in the likeness of his death" (Rom. 6:3-5).

IV. Jesus Is the Son of God.

A. Voices from Heaven acknowledged the person of Christ at His birth, His baptism, His transfiguration, and during the concluding days of His ministry.
B. At His baptism, Jesus was honored by the Spirit and the Father!
C. God declares that Jesus is the Son of God (Matt. 3:17).
D. Here the Father states that which John so often spoke (John 1:1-14).
E. John 20:31
F. The church of our Lord is founded upon this fundamental proposition (Matt. 16:15-18).
G. It was said in Matthew 14:33, "Of a truth thou art the Son of God."

Conclusion

Won't you come fulfilling the righteousness of God and be baptized, not into John's baptism, but into Christ for the remission of your sins?

"They That Were Ready"

Introduction

1. Matthew 25:1-13
2. The Scriptures place importance upon being ready.

Discussion

I. Ready to Hear.

A. Ecclesiastes 5:1-2
B. James 1:19
C. Ready to hear Christ (Matt. 17:5). He hath the words of life (John 6:63, 68).
D. Ready to hear the Word of God (Acts 13:7). Faith comes by hearing (Rom. 10:17).

II. Ready to Preach the Gospel.

A. Romans 1:15-17
B. Paul's charge to Timothy (2 Tim. 4:1-5).
C. Christ commanded that the gospel be preached to every creature (Mark 16:15).
D. The gospel saves (Rom. 1:16), but it must first be preached (1 Cor. 1:21).

III. Ready to Every Good Work.

A. Tit. 3:1
B. 2 Timothy 2:21
C. Good works are the responsibility of every Christian (Eph. 2:10; Tit. 2:14; 3:8).
D. Good works cause others to glorify God (Matt. 5:16).

IV. Ready Always to Give an Answer.

A. 1 Peter 3:15
B. Colossians 4:6
C. This emphasizes the importance of diligent, daily Bible study (2 Tim. 2:15).

V. Ready to Distribute.

A. 1 Timothy 6:18

B. We are taught to distribute to the necessity of saints (Rom. 12:13).

C. Early disciples distributed to the needs of others (Acts 4:34-35).

D. We need to be liberal in our distribution (2 Cor. 9:13).

VI. Ready to Die.

A. Psalm 88:15

B. Acts 21:13

C. Death will come to all.

1. 1 Corinthians 15:22
2. Hebrews 9:27

D. Are you ready to die?

VII. Ready for the Coming of the Son of Man.

A. Matthew 24:42-44

B. Christ will come again.

1. John 14:1-3
2. Hebrews 9:28

C. Christ will come unexpectedly.

1. Mark 13:32
2. 2 Peter 3:10

D. Will He find you ready?

Conclusion

1. ". . . they that were ready went in with him" (Matt. 25:10).
2. Are you ready?

Spiritual Be Not's

Introduction

1. "Be not" are two words designed to teach us some valuable spiritual lessons.
2. A good companion lesson is "Bible Be's."
3. Let's notice some *be not's*.

Discussion

I. Be Not Many Masters/Teachers.

A. James 3:1
B. Heavier judgment – this has nothing to do with degrees of punishments or rewards.
C. The greater the opportunity and ability is the responsibility and judgment.

II. Be Not Wise in Your Own Conceits.

A. Romans 12:16; 11:25
B. None superior to other Christians.
C. Must not let our opinions override the Scriptures.
D. Jeremiah 10:23
E. Romans 12:3
F. Galatians 6:3

III. Be Not Children in Understanding.

A. 1 Corinthians 14:20
B. Ephesians 3:3-5
C. 1 Corinthians 14:2, 15-16
D. Colossians 1:9

IV. Be Not Unequally Yoked.

A. 2 Corinthians 6:14
B. Discuss 2 Corinthians 6:14-18

V. Be Not Partakers With Them.

A. Ephesians 5:7

B. Discuss Ephesians 5:3-7

VI. Be Not Drunk.

A. Ephesians 5:18
B. Proverbs 20:1
C. Drinking is a sin in that "banquetings" are condemned (1 Pet. 4:3).
D. Galatians 5:19-21 shows one of the works of the flesh is that of drunkenness.

VII. Be Not Unwise.

A. Ephesians 5:17
B. The unwise are not acceptable with God.
C. Romans 1:14 speaks of both the wise and unwise.

VIII. Let It Not Be the Outward Adorning.

A. 1 Peter 3:3
B. Peter is contrasting the outward and inward man with emphasis on the inner man (1 Pet. 3:1-5).
C. 2 Corinthians 4:16-18

Conclusion

There is something we must be and that is a child of God (Gal. 3:26-27).

Worry

Introduction

1. We live life in the fast lane. There is always too much to do and too little time. There are problems everywhere. The result for many is worry.
2. Stress is really our number one health problem.
3. Jesus' prescription for worry – Matthew 6:23-33.

Discussion

I. Life Is More Than the Physical.

A. Matthew 6:25

B. Dr. Robert Elliott said, "Rule #1 — Don't sweat the small stuff. Rule #2 – It's all small stuff!"

C. Recognize what's really important, your soul, not the material things of life.

II. God Will Care for You.

A. Matthew 6:26, 28-30

B. Worry comes from a lack of faith.

C. As God has provided for nature, He will take care of His own.

D. Psalm 23; 2 Timothy 1:7-8

III. Worry Does No Good.

A. Matthew 6:27

B. "Worry is like a rocking chair. It will give you something to do, but it won't get you anywhere."

C. What changes by worry? What problem does it solve?

D. Often worrying is a method of absorbing time in place of positive activity.

E. Worrying about the past is a waste of spirit (Phil. 3:13-14).

IV. Seek God First.

A. Matthew 6:33

B. We often worry because of sin in our lives. We know we are not ready to die.

C. Philippians 1:21-24; Acts 24:25

V. Live One Day at a Time.

A. Matthew 6:34

B. Some people experience trouble three times. First in anticipation, second in actual realization, and third in living it over and over again.

C. Mark Twain – "I've known a lot of troubles in my life, and most of them never happened!" "Man is too prone to worry about what he thinks is going to happen."

D. We don't know what the future holds (Jas. 1:12-14). Just take one day at a time.

Conclusion

1. Prayer will help us deal with worry (Phil. 4:6-7; 1 Pet. 5:7).
2. God's Word gives us great comfort and peace (Rom. 15:4).

Good Attitudes Needed Today

Introduction

1. Attitude is important. The Bible says, "For as he thinketh in his heart, so is he" (Prov. 23:7).
2. Let's notice some things that demonstrate a good attitude; such as are sorely needed today.

Discussion

I. Philip's Running.

A. Acts 8:30

B. Philip's running after the man from Ethiopia demonstrated his enthusiasm for teaching the truth.

C. How many of us would run to teach someone?

D. His running paid off as Philip baptized the eunuch (Acts 8:38) and the eunuch went on his way rejoicing (Acts 8:39).

E. This is an attitude that we need to cultivate among ourselves!

II. Isaiah's "Here Am I; Send Me."

A. As God commissioned Isaiah, the Scriptures say, "Also I heard the voice of the Lord saying, Whom shall I send, and who will go for us? Then said I, Here am I; send me" (Isa. 6:8).

B. "Here am I; send me" is an attitude badly needed today among God's people. It would seem that we would prefer for God to send someone else!

C. Song: "There Is Much to Do."

D. Each one needs to be involved in the Lord's work!

III. Job's "Though He Slay Me, Yet Will I Trust in Him."

A. Job 13:15

B. This is an attitude of complete and absolute trust.

C. Job's trust was based upon the fact that he knew that, if he were to die, he would live on (Job 14:14).

D. Will we trust in God no matter what may happen to us in this life?

E. Job's restoration is recorded in chapter 42 and the ". . . Lord blessed the latter end of Job more than his beginning. . ." (Job 42:12).

IV. Joshua's "For Me and My House, We Will Serve the Lord."

A. Joshua 24:15

B. The people on this occasion said, ". . . we will serve the Lord" (Josh. 24:21).

C. We need this attitude today! The attitude that, in spite of what others may or may not do, we will be found serving God!

D. Serving God is something that each one of us must determine to do. Nobody can serve the Lord for you!

E. It's difficult to stand against the crowd and do the right thing, but the reward for such will be eternal life!

F. We sing, "Stand up, stand up for Jesus! The strife will not be long; This day the noise of battle, The next the victor's song."

V. Paul's "I Can Do All Things."

A. Philippians 4:13

B. "I can" is a stepping stone to success while "I can't" is but the stepping stone to failure!

C. Thomas Edison didn't know the meaning of "I can't" as he failed 6,000 times before he found the right material for the filament of his light bulb.

D. Here the Lord is promising strength to enable us to overcome every circumstance.

E. Relying on the strength which Christ provides, we have full assurance that we can win the victory!

Conclusion

How's your attitude?

Divine Rules and Their Exceptions

Introduction

1. There are rules and there are exceptions to the rules.
2. In spelling, the letter "i" comes before the letter "e" except after the letter "c".
3. Let's notice some divine rules and their exceptions.

Discussion

I. The Rule Is Christ Has All Authority.

A. Christ has all authority.
   1. Matthew 7:29
   2. Matthew 28:18
   3. Ephesians 1:21-23

B. God is the exception to the rule (1 Cor. 15:27-28; 11:3).

C. We must submit unto Christ (Phil. 2:9-11).

II. The Rule Is Marriage Is for Life.

A. Marriage is a life-long commitment.
   1. Romans 7:1-4
   2. 1 Corinthians 7:39
   3. Matthew 19:6

B. The Lord added fornication as being the only exception to this divine rule (Matt. 19:9; 5:32).

III. The Rule Is Death Will Pass Upon All.

A. Death will pass upon all.
   1. Ecclesiastes 9:5
   2. Job 30:23
   3. Romans 5:12
   4. 1 Corinthians 15:22
   5. Hebrews 9:27

B. Enoch was an exception to this divine rule (Gen. 5:22-24; Heb. 11:5).
C. Elijah was an exception (2 Kings 2:11).
D. Those living when Christ returns will be excepted (1 Cor. 15:51-53; 1 Thess. 4:15-17).

IV. The Rule Is All Will Resurrect at the Last Day.

A. There will be a resurrection of all the dead at the last day (John 5:28-29; 11:24; Acts 24:15).
B. Christ is the exception to this rule (Matt. 28:6).
C. He is the only one that resurrected to never die again.
D. He is the firstfruits (1 Cor. 15:20).

V. The Rule Is All Have Sinned.

A. Sin is universal in that all are guilty.
   1. Romans 3:9
   2. Romans 3:23
   3. Galatians 3:22
   4. 1 John 1:8
B. Jesus Christ is the one exception to this rule.
   1. Luke 23:41
   2. 2 Corinthians 5:21
   3. Hebrews 4:15
   4. 1 Peter 2:22
C. We are under the rule and must have our sins pardoned.

VI. The Rule Is Sinners Punished at Judgment.

A. Sinners will be punished at the judgment.
   1. Hebrews 9:27
   2. 2 Corinthians 5:10
   3. Romans 14:10
B. Ananias and Sapphira were an exception (Acts 5:1-11).
C. Are you prepared for the judgment?

Conclusion

1. Here are six divine rules and their exceptions.
2. Do not depend upon the Lord making any exceptions to His rules of salvation.
3. Obey right now!

Some Things Jesus Was Found Doing

Introduction

1. Jesus "went about doing good. . ." (Acts 10:38).
2. He was always doing something.
3. Thus, we take a look at some things He was found doing.

Discussion

I. Paying His Taxes.

A. Matthew 17:24-27

B. So must we (Rom. 13:1-6).

C. Mary and Joseph went to be taxed (Luke 2).

II. Washing the Feet of the Disciples.

A. John 13:1-17

1. Purpose was to teach humility.
2. This was not an act of worship.
3. Foot washing was in the class of good works (1 Tim. 5:10).

B. We must be engaged in good works (Gal. 6:10).

III. Performing Miracles.

A. Walked on water (John 6:19).

B. John 6:5-14; 5:1-12; 9:7

C. Purpose of His miracles was to cause people to believe.

1. John 2:22
2. John 4:39-41
3. John 6:2, 14

IV. Setting a Good Example.

A. 1 Peter 2:21

B. Good to know what Jesus would have done.

V. Rebuking False Teachers.

A. His most severe condemnation was to false teachers.

1. Matthew 23
2. Matthew 7:15

B. We must be able to do such (1 John 4:1).

VI. Weeping.

A. John 11:35, 33-38; Matthew 9:36-38

B. We must never become too hardened or too big to cry!

VII. Bearing Our Sins.

A. Isaiah 53:4-7

B. 1 Peter 2:24

Conclusion

1. We need to hear, believe, and obey the gospel of our Lord.
2. You may come now as we sing.

"Teach Us to Number Our Days"

Introduction

1. Psalm 90:12
2. After contrasting God's eternal and powerful nature with man, who is weak and transitory, this is David's conclusion.

Discussion

I. "Teach Us."

A. We should desire teaching from God's Word. Many don't today.

B. Acts 8:30-31; 1 Peter 2:2

C. Surveys indicate that only 11% of Americans read their Bible daily. We have a society who claim some belief in the Bible, but is basically ignorant of what it teaches.

II. "To Number Our Days."

A. He tells you to do what you cannot! We don't know when we are going to die, so we don't know how many days we have left!

B. He means:

1. Realize life passes rapidly (Ps. 90:5-6, 9-10; Job 14:1-2).
2. Realize you can lose your life at any time (1 Sam. 20:3).
3. Death will come (Heb. 9:27; Eccl. 9:5).

C. Some act as if they are going to live forever!

D. Live everyday as if it were your last and someday not only will you be right, but you will also be ready!

III. "That We May Apply Our Hearts unto Wisdom."

A. Live wisely.

B. Colossians 4:5; Ecclesiastes 8:5; Ephesians 5:15-16

C. Time is precious and shouldn't be wasted.

D. We should view life as a whole, as if we were at the end of it and looking back. What would we change? Do that now and live wisely.

E. To apply our hearts to wisdom is to realize that some things are more important than others – God, family, others, etc.

F. "Many of us spend our lives chasing rainbows, that even if we could catch them, would be worthless to us."

G. Matthew 6:33

H. Don't let the things that are urgent day by day crowd out the important things of life, or you may one day wake up and find you have wasted most of your life on trivialities.

Conclusion

1. Ecclesiastes 7:2 – Going to a funeral can be beneficial. We may be caused to seriously consider our own death and then to reflect upon how we are living.
2. Are you living wisely?

"Under Whose Wings Thou Art Come to Trust"

Introduction

1. Text: Ruth 2:12
2. The virtuous Ruth left the land of her nativity (Moab) and came unto the people of God and said, "thy people shall be my people, and thy God my God" (Ruth 1:16). She had come, through the good influence of her family and especially her mother-in-law, Naomi, to trust in Jehovah God. As a result of her trust and obedience, she became a descendant of the Messiah.
3. We would do well to come to trust under God's wings, even as the chicks gather under the wings of the hen (Matt. 23:37).
4. Let's notice some who trusted in God.

Discussion

I. Job Trusted in God.

A. Job 13:15-16

B. Even though Job was receiving evil, he would not blame God or charge God foolishly (Job 2:7-10).

C. Some think that trusting in God means that no evil will ever come to them. This is certainly not true as we can see in Job's case.

1. Paul said, "yea, and all that will live godly in Christ Jesus shall suffer persecution" (2 Tim. 3:12).
2. All things will work out for God's purposes (Rom. 8:28).

D. Job 19:25-26

E. Oh, if we could only have the trust of Job!

II. David Trusted in God.

A. Notice David's song of praise when he was delivered out of the hand of his enemies (2 Sam. 22:1-7).

B. David trusted in God as his shield, horn of salvation, high tower (stronghold), refuge, and saviour.

C. Many of David's psalms speak of trusting in God (Pss. 4:5; 5:11; 7:1; 9:10; 11:1; 16:1; 18:2; 25:1-2, 20; 31:1; 34:22; 36:7; 37:40).

D. It was God who put away David's sin in the case of his sin with Bathsheba (2 Sam. 12:13). Notice David's psalm written after Nathan the prophet came unto him, after he had gone in to Bathsheba (Ps. 51).

E. David exemplified his trust in God in the death of his son by Bathsheba when he said, "I shall go to him" (2 Sam. 12:23).

III. Shadrach, Meshach, and Abednego Trusted in God.

A. Relate story of Daniel 3 and Nebuchadnezzar's image.

B. Notice their trust in God (Dan. 3:17-18).

C. The fourth form in the fire was like the Son of God (Dan. 3:25). That's what God did for them when they put their complete trust in Him.

IV. Paul Trusted in God.

A. 1 Timothy 4:10

B. Remember Paul's trouble in Asia (2 Cor. 1:8-11).

C. He trusted in God so much that he looked for a crown of righteousness (2 Tim. 4:6-8).

D. Paul suffered many things (2 Cor. 11:23-28), but he always looked to the Lord (2 Tim. 4:18).

E. In the case of his thorn in the flesh, Paul had come to trust in God (2 Cor. 12:7-10).

Conclusion

1. Where have you put your trust?
2. Is your trust in "the living God, who giveth us richly all things to enjoy" (1 Tim. 6:17)?
3. Is your trust an innocent, unequivocal, complete, absolute trust in God (Ps. 2:12)?

Bible Runners

Introduction

1. The Bible catalogues several individuals who ran.
2. The fact that they ran shows their interest and eagerness in serving the Lord.
3. Let's call attention to some who ran.

Discussion

I. Joseph Ran.

A. Genesis 39:12

B. Joseph ran from the temptation to sin!

C. A lot of people succumb to temptation because of tarrying (2 Sam. 11:1-4).

D. The Bible teaches us to flee (1 Cor. 6:18; 2 Tim. 2:22).

II. The Man with an Unclean Spirit Ran.

A. Mark 5:6

B. This man ran to worship the Lord!

C. One of God's greatest blessings to man is that of worship.

D. We should be interested and eager to worship the Lord (John 4:24; 1 Chron. 16:29)!

III. The Rich Young Ruler Ran.

A. Mark 10:17

B. This man ran to learn about how to have eternal life!

C. He had a problem on his mind. He had not found that which would put his soul to rest.

D. We need to realize that we are lost and be eager to learn how to be saved (Acts 2:37; 16:30).

IV. Zacchaeus Ran.

A. Luke 19:4

B. Zacchaeus ran to see Jesus!

C. Some today will never see Jesus because they allow too many things to get in their way.

D. Remove the barriers that keep you from seeing Jesus!

V. Philip Ran.

A. Acts 8:30

B. Philip ran to teach a person about Christ!

C. This brought about the conversion of the Ethiopian eunuch (Acts 8:36-39).

D. We are taught to teach (2 Tim. 2:2; 1 Tim. 4:16).

E. How eager are you to teach others about Jesus Christ?

VI. Paul Ran.

A. 1 Corinthians 9:24-27

B. Life is compared to running a race (Heb. 12:1-2).

C. Paul entered the race of life and finished the course (2 Tim. 4:7).

D. Will you enter the race?

Conclusion

1. Here are some men who ran.
2. Have you ever run in doing the will of God?

Some Things Jesus Was Seen Doing

Introduction

1. Jesus was a busy man while He was here on Earth (Acts 1:1; John 21:25).
2. Notice some things Jesus was seen doing.

Discussion

I. Being About His Father's Business.

A. Luke 2:49

B. John 2:16

C. John 6:38-39

1. Hebrews 10:4-10
2. John 4:34

II. Being Subject to His Parents.

A. Luke 2:51

B. A great need of today (Eph. 6:1-2).

III. Growing.

A. Luke 2:52

B. Please note the four areas in which Jesus grew.

1. He was well-rounded.
2. We must grow as He did.

IV. Quoting Scripture.

A. Jesus resisted the temptations of Satan by remembering and quoting Scripture (Matt. 4:1-11).

B. Psalm 119:11 – By hiding God's Word in our hearts we have a good defense against sin.

V. Praying.

A. Matthew 26:36-42

B. John 20:30-3
C. Philippians 4:6; 1 Thessalonians 5:17; Ephesians 6:18

VI. Attending a Wedding.

A. John 2:1-2 – Jesus recognized and approved of marriage.
B. Hebrews 13:4
C. Marriage is as old as Adam and Eve (Gen. 2:18-24).
D. When invited it's good to take your children and attend a wedding to encourage the young to marry scripturally.

VII. Instituting the Lord's Supper.

A. Few men institute their own memorials. But, Jesus did!
B. Matthew 26:26-29; 1 Corinthians 11:23-24
C. We must observe this memorial today in His memory and on the first day of the week (Acts 20:7).

VIII. Teaching.

A. Jesus was the Master Teacher!
B. Acts 1:1; John 8:1-2; 3:2
C. Much of His teaching was done by parables.

Conclusion

1. Our Lord was seen being baptized (Matt. 3:16).
2. How about you? Will you be seen being baptized?

Things I Wish Were True

Introduction

1. We have all sat around and daydreamed about things we might like to have or do, or if we were in charge how things would be done.
2. Well I'm afraid when it comes to religion many people have done a lot of wishful thinking about what they believe is true.
3. If I had my "ruthers," I might wish these.

Discussion

I. Saved by Faith Only.

A. Many people believe this.
B. It would be nice to believe. It would save so many.
C. But it is wishful thinking – it is not true.
D. James 2:24; Matthew 7:21
E. Saul was told what he had to do to be saved (Acts 9:6), which included being baptized (Acts 22:16).

II. The Bible Cannot Be Understood.

A. Many believe it cannot.
B. It would be nice – wouldn't have to study.
C. The Bible can be understood, and we are commanded to read and understand it!
D. Ephesians 3:3-4; 5:17; 2 Timothy 2:15

III. Sin Wasn't Really Harmful.

A. Many act like sin doesn't hurt anything. They sin without remorse.
B. Wouldn't this be nice if it were true? You could do anything you wanted.
C. Sin is hurtful!
D. Sin separates from God (Isa. 59:2).
E. Sin eventually will lead us to be lost in hell (Rom. 6:23; 1 Cor. 6:9-11).
F. Jesus died to take away sin.

IV. The Church Was Unimportant.

A. Many believe it isn't important. They don't attend, and they think salvation can be found without it.
B. You wouldn't have to worry about getting up on Sunday for church or giving to it.
C. But this is just wishful thinking!
D. The church is important!
E. Christ died for it (Acts 20:28).
F. It is Christ's body (Col. 1:18).
G. It's the saved (Eph. 5:23; Acts 2:47).

V. There Is No Hell.

A. Many deny its existence.
B. If there is no hell, you wouldn't have to worry about God, or judgment, or how you live.
C. But there is a hell – a place of eternal punishment for the wicked.
D. Matthew 25:41, 46; 2 Thessalonians 1:7-9
E. Therefore, we need to obey God and be saved that we may go to Heaven.

VI. There Will Be a Second Chance after Death.

A. Many believe that God will give those sincerely ignorant another chance.
B. It would be nice, wouldn't it?
C. It isn't true! We will be judged based on the way we live here on the earth (2 Cor. 5:10; Rom. 2:6).
D. After death, our fate is sealed and there is no change (Luke 16 – great gulf fixed).
E. We must serve God now while we have the time and opportunity.

Conclusion

1. Wishing these things does not make them true!
2. Let us always believe and preach the truth (Gal. 4:16; John 8:32).

Those in Danger of Hell Fire

Introduction

1. Text: Matthew 5:22
2. Jesus emphasized that there are those who are in danger of hell fire. Who is it?

Discussion

I. Those Angry Without Just Cause.

- A. While the Bible does not condemn anger per se, it does condemn anger without just cause (Matt. 5:22).
- B. Jesus taught that to be angry with a brother without a just cause is enough to cause one to be in danger, danger of judgment, and even hell fire!
- C. Anger associated with a just cause is not condemned (Eph. 4:26; Mark 3:5; John 2:15; Jas. 1:19).
- D. "Ra'ca" (*ra'-cah*) is a Jewish term of disrespect that means "emptyhead" or "stupid."
- E. "Raca" and "fool" represent states of unrighteous anger for which an account must be given (Matt. 12:36).
- F. 1 John 3:15
- G. ". . . We ought also to love one another" (1 John 4:11).

II. Those Who Have Not Disciplined Their Eyes, Hands, and Feet.

- A. Those who have not disciplined such have offending body members.
- B. Offending body members will cause the whole body to be cast into hell (Matt. 5:29-30).
  1. Offending eyes (Matt. 5:29; 18:9; Mark 9:47).
  2. Offending hands (Matt. 5:30; Mark 9:43).
  3. Offending feet (Mark 9:45).
- C. Jesus is not commanding mutilation, but mortification (discipline)!
  1. Behave as if you had actually plucked out your eyes and could not see the object which previously caused you to sin. Behave as if you had actually cut off your hands and feet, and were now crippled and could

not do the things or visit the places which previously caused you to sin!
2. This is what mortification is all about!

D. We must put sinful practices to death (Mark 8:34; Rom. 8:13; Gal. 5:24; Col. 3:5).
E. We must eliminate sources of temptation (Jas. 1:14-15; Gal. 5:19-21).

III. Hypocrites.

A. Matthew 23:33
B. We learn much about hypocrisy in Matthew 23.
   1. We learn what it is (Matt. 23:3, 25).
   2. We learn its motive (Matt. 23:5).
   3. We learn what actions constitute hypocrisy (Matt. 23:13-33).
   4. We learn its consequences (Matt. 23:33).
C. Hypocrites are the children of hell! (Matt. 23:15).
D. The hypocrite's heart is far from God (Matt. 15:7) which makes his worship vain (Matt. 15:9).
E. Job 8:13
F. Hypocrites "have their reward" (Matt. 6:2, 5, 16).
G. The hypocrite can make needed correction by casting the beam out of his own eye (Matt. 7:5) and by laying hypocrisy aside (1 Pet. 2:1).

IV. Those Who Forget God and Others.

A. Luke 16:19-25 – This man was not in danger of hell fire, he was in hell fire (Luke 16:23-24)!
B. The rich man whose ground ". . . brought forth plentifully" thought only of himself (Luke 12:16-21).
C. Song "Others" says, "Others, Lord, yes others, let this my motto be, help me to live for others, that I may live like thee" (Matt. 25:45-46).
D. God will take vengeance on them that know Him not (2 Thess. 1:8-9).
E. Romans 14:7

V. Those Not in Christ.

A. 2 Timothy 2:10; 3:15
B. If salvation is in Christ, then what will the end be of those who are not in Christ?
C. God purposed salvation in Christ even before the foundation of the world (2 Tim. 1:9).
D. Romans 3:24; 1 Corinthians 15:22-24
E. Paul taught that we are children of God in Christ, must be baptized into Christ to put on Christ, and as Christ's we are made heirs (Gal. 3:26-29).
F. No need to remain outside of Christ as we've been invited to Him (Matt. 11:28-30).

VI. The Young Who Don't Remember Their Creator or Honor Their Parents.

A. Ecclesiastes 12:1

B. The young will be brought into judgment and must therefore put away evil (Eccl. 11:9).

C. Ecclesiastes 12:13-14

D. Children, out of obedience to the Almighty, are called upon to honor their parents and obey them (Eph. 6:1-2) that it may be well with them, and they may live long upon the Earth (Eph. 6:3; Col. 3:20).

E. The young need to cleanse their way by taking heed to God's Word (Ps. 119:9).

F. 1 Timothy 4:12

VII. False Teachers Among Us.

A. 2 Peter 2:1-9

B. Just as God "spared not the angels that sinned, but cast them down to hell" (2 Pet. 2:4), such will be the end of those who espouse false doctrine!

C. We must ". . . beware of false prophets" which come in sheep's clothing (Matt. 7:15), for they can transform themselves into "an angel of light" (2 Cor. 11:14).

D. There will be those who will ". . . corrupt the word of God" (2 Cor. 2:17).

E. Those who preach "another gospel" will be accursed, a thing devoted to God for destruction! (Gal. 1:6-8).

VIII. Indifferent Christians.

A. Christ warned the Laodicean Christians about their indifferent attitude and told them He would spue them out of His mouth (Rev. 3:14-16).

B. These lukewarm, unzealous, indifferent Christians were in grave danger, danger of hell fire, and were told to repent of their wrong doing (Rev. 3:19).

C. The Christians at Ephesus had left their first love and were told to repent and do the first works; OR ELSE! (Rev. 3:4-5).

D. God's people must never be indifferent or apathetic, but be ". . . always abounding in the work of the Lord. . ." (1 Cor. 15:58).

E. Those who won't attend, pray, sing, study, give, observe the Lord's supper, work, etc. are in danger of hell fire!

F. Christians must practice faith and works! (Jas. 2:17, 24).

G. Paul taught the Roman Christians, "And that, knowing the time, that now it is high time to awake out of sleep: for now is our salvation nearer than when we believed" (Rom. 13:11). He might have said, ". . . for now is hell fire nearer than when we believed!"

Conclusion

1. Jesus' question ". . . how can ye escape the damnation of hell?" (Matt. 23:33) implies that hell fire can be escaped or avoided.

2. Matthew 10:28
3. Won't you come fearing God and keeping His commandments, knowing that to do otherwise is to be in danger of hell fire?

A Five Second Sermon

Introduction

1. I am going to preach a five second sermon.
2. This sermon has nothing to do with the length of a sermon, but rather with five different seconds mentioned in the Bible.

Discussion

I. Second Covenant.

A. Hebrews 8:7
B. An everlasting covenant (Isa. 55:3; Heb. 13:20).
C. A better covenant (Heb. 7:22).
   1. Established upon better promises (Heb. 8:6).
   2. Has better sacrifices (Heb. 9:23).
   3. Brings a better hope (Heb. 7:19).
D. The mediator is Christ (Heb. 8:6; 12:24).
E. Ushered into force by Christ's death (Heb. 9:15-17).
F. Covenant by which we are sanctified (Heb. 10:9-10).

II. Second Commandment.

A. Matthew 22:39
B. Notice the love the good Samaritan had for his neighbor (Luke 10:25-37).
C. This love requires that we do no ill to our neighbor (Rom. 13:9-10).
D. When we love our neighbor as we ought, we fulfill the law (Jas. 2:8-9).
E. A proper love for our neighbor will cause us to teach him the gospel (2 Tim. 2:2).

III. Second Man.

A. 1 Corinthians 15:47
B. Adam was the first man (1 Cor. 15:45). He brought death (1 Cor. 15:22).
C. Christ is the second man (1 Cor. 15:47). He brought life (1 Cor. 15:22; 1 John 5:11).
D. Have you submitted unto the will of Christ?

IV. Second Coming.

A. Hebrews 9:28

B. Christ has promised to come again (John 14:1-3).

C. He will come as He left (Acts 1:9-11).

D. He will come unexpectedly (Mark 13:32; 2 Pet. 3:10).

E. He will come to reward the faithful and punish the disobedient (Matt. 16:27; 2 Thess. 1:7-9).

V. Second Death.

A. The Bible often speaks of the second death.

1. Romans 6:23
2. Revelation 2:11
3. Revelation 20:6
4. Revelation 20:14

B. The second death will be an eternal separation from God in a place of torment.

C. Notice some individuals who will experience the second death (Rev. 21:8).

Conclusion

1. Here are five different seconds mentioned in the Bible.
2. Obey now as we stand and sing!

"Sir, We Would See Jesus"

Introduction

1. There are a lot of great men we would like to see.
2. Men desired to see Jesus while He was here on Earth (John 12:20-21).
3. What did men see when they saw Jesus?

Discussion

I. They Saw the Son of God.

A. Thomas saw Jesus and said, "My Lord and my God" (John 12:28).
B. Jesus was God/man (John 1:3, 14).
C. He was Christ, the Lord (Luke 2:11).
D. His coming to the Earth did not make Him any less God than before He came.

II. John Saw the Lamb of God.

A. John 1:29; Isaiah 53:7
B. The Lamb of the New Testament could do what the lamb of the Old Testament could not do, take away sin!

III. Stephen Saw Jesus on God's Right Hand.

A. Some deny that Jesus is on God's right hand.
B. Just ask Stephen (Acts 7:56).
C. Colossians 3:1

IV. The Author and Finisher of Our Faith.

A. Hebrews 12:1-2; 5:8-9
B. But, we must obey Him!

V. Some Saw Him Dying.

A. John 19:37; Zechariah 12:10
B. Hebrews 2:9; Luke 23:35; Matthew 27:35-36
C. The Crucified One!

Conclusion

1. Micah 7:7
2. Come, and obey this Saviour as we sing.

Our Giving unto the Lord

Introduction

1. The Lord has planned for financing the work of the church. This is done by the giving of its members.
2. It's important to understand our individual responsibilities regarding giving.

Discussion

I. Giving Is a Divine Command.

A. 1 Corinthians 16:1-2 – ". . . As I have given order. . . ."

B. There is authority for a treasury, inasmuch as they were to lay by in store and the gathering was to be done before Paul arrived (1 Cor. 16:2).

C. Early church practiced giving regularly into treasury and had resources to spend:

1. Preaching (Phil. 4).
2. Benevolence (Acts 11).

D. Luke 6:38; 2 Corinthians 9:7; Acts 20:35

E. Need to work so as to be able to provide for family, help others, and give to the Lord's church.

II. All Christians Are to Give.

A. 1 Corinthians 16:2 – ". . . let every one of you. . . ."

B. 2 Corinthians 9:7 – "Every man. . . ."

C. Each member of the church is to give.

D. This applies to all Christians and was not just to the wealthy.

III. Motives Behind Our Giving.

A. We often look at cashflow out of pocket rather than rich benefits which come to us as a result of our giving.

B. Why should we give?

1. To obey God (1 Cor. 16:2; Rev. 22:15).
2. God blesses the giver (Acts 20:32; 2 Cor. 9:7; Luke 6:38).
3. To support work of the church (1 Tim. 3:15).

4. To lay up treasures in Heaven (Matt. 6:19-20; 1 Tim. 6:17-19; Phil. 4:15-19).
5. Proves our sincerity (2 Cor. 8:8).

IV. We Are to Give as Purposed.

A. 2 Corinthians 9:7

B. "Purposeth" means to plan ahead; give with deliberate forethought and intention.

C. Giving needs to be "off the top."

D. Too many get into debt and then can't give.

V. Must Give with Right Attitude.

A. Attitude is important in all we do.

B. Some negate the benefits of giving because they don't have right attitude.

C. Good attitudes:

1. Gave of prosperity or giving as we have received of the Lord (1 Cor. 16:2; 2 Cor. 8:12).
2. Gave generously (Rom. 12:8; 2 Cor. 8:12; 9:6).
3. Gave sacrificially (Mark 12:41-44; Mal. 3:8-10).

VI. The Example of the Macedonians.

A. 2 Corinthians 8:1-5

B. See reflected what we have been discussing.

1. Grace bestowed (2 Cor. 8:1).
2. Gave of their joy (2 Cor. 8:2).
3. Made sacrifice (2 Cor. 8:3).
4. Attitude – ". . . willing of themselves" (2 Cor. 8:3).
5. Considered it a favor if allowed to give (2 Cor. 8:4).
6. Gave out of commitment to Jesus (2 Cor. 8:5).

C. How do we compare with this great example?

Conclusion

As stewards, we must be faithful (1 Cor. 4:2).

“Come . . . and See My Zeal for the Lord”

Introduction

1. Text: 2 Kings 10:16
2. In 2 Kings 10, we find Je-hon-a-dab joining with King Jehu of Israel to rid Israel of Baal worship. Jehu told Jehonadab to “come . . . and see my zeal for the Lord” (2 Kings 10:16).
3. Zeal – “enthusiastic devotion for a cause, an ideal, or a goal and tireless diligence in its furtherance” (AHD).

Discussion

I. A Number of Bible Passages Speak of Zeal.

- A. These Bible passages will give us a better appreciation of what zeal is. Read and carefully study each passage and its context.
- B. Psalm 69:9; John 2:12-17
- C. Romans 10:1-2
- D. 2 Corinthians 7:9-11
- E. 2 Corinthians 9:2
- F. Philippians 3:6; Acts 9:2; 22:3-4

II. Some Areas in Which We Need Zeal.

- A. **Zeal for preaching the gospel of Christ.**
    1. Mark 16:15-16
    2. The book of Acts is the carrying out of this commission (Acts 1:8).
    3. Philip’s zeal is clearly seen in Acts 8:30.
    4. Paul’s zeal for the preaching of the gospel is seen in his preaching trips throughout Asia, Greece, and Rome.
    5. Romans 1:16
    6. Paul preached the gospel (1 Cor. 15:1-4).
- B. **Zeal in the worship of God.**

1. Much worship today lacks zeal!
2. John 4:24 – ". . . in spirit and in truth."
3. "Behold, what a weariness is it" (Mal. 1:13).
4. Worship must come from the heart, and be offered with enthusiasm (Matt. 15:8).

C. **Zeal in not forsaking the assembling.**
1. Hebrews 10:25
2. Can your zeal for the Lord be seen in your eagerness to assemble with God's people?
3. Paul tarried at Troas so as to be able to assemble with God's people (Acts 20:6-7).
4. What if each member's attendance was just like your attendance?

D. **Zeal in our singing.**
1. Ephesians 5:19; Colossians 3:16
2. Notice the "I will sing" in Hebrews 2:12.
3. Singing is an expression of our heart and our hearts should be merry (Jas. 5:13).

E. **Zeal in doing all by the Lord's authority.**
1. Colossians 3:17; Matthew 28:18
2. Much today is being done without the Lord's authority!
3. We must ". . . speak as the oracles of God" (1 Pet. 4:11).

F. **Zeal in putting the Lord first in our lives.**
1. Matthew 6:33
2. Far too many people are putting other things before the Lord!

Conclusion

1. We need a good dose of zeal.
2. It is said, in the book of Luke, of the early disciples, their heart burned within them (Luke 24:32). Something turned these timid and fearful disciples into a force that could not be quenched, their zeal.

Men Without Regard for God

Introduction

1. Psalm 54
2. We take a look at some men without regard for God.

Discussion

I. Men Who Say There Is No God.

A. Some do not believe there is a God.

B. The Bible holds God up as being in existence (Gen. 1:1; Pss. 19:1; 90:1-2; Acts 17:28; Heb. 11:6).

C. Only a fool declares there is no God (Ps. 14:1).

II. Men Who Do Not Trust in God.

A. Some do not have firm reliance on God.

B. Men who have regard for God, trust in God.

1. Job 13:15
2. Psalm 62:5-8
3. 1 Timothy 4:10
4. 1 Timothy 6:17

C. Have you put your trust in God?

III. Men Who Do Not Love God.

A. Many do not love God as they should.

B. Mark 12:30

C. 1 Corinthians 8:3

D. Loving God involves keeping the commandments of God (1 John 5:3).

E. Loving God involves having love for the children of God (1 John 4:20-21).

IV. Men Who Sin Against God.

A. To sin against God is to transgress the law of God (1 John 3:4).

B. Sin against God is a serious thing!

1. Romans 6:23

2. Isaiah 59:1-2
3. Hebrews 10:26

C. When we sin against God, we need to make it right with God!

V. Men Who Resist the Powers Ordained of God.

A. Ecclesiastes 8:2
B. We show regard for God by submitting to the civil government which is appointed by God.
C. Romans 13:1-7
D. 1 Peter 2:13-14
E. When government is out of its place, we ought to obey God (Acts 5:29).

VI. Men Who Take in Vain the Name of God.

A. The name of God is holy and reverend (Ps. 111:9).
B. Those who take the name of God in vain will be punished (Exod. 20:7; Lev. 24:10-16).
C. We must hallow God's name (Lev. 22:32; Matt. 6:9).

VII. Men Who Do Not Obey God.

A. We ought to obey God (Acts 5:29).
B. Those who do not obey will be punished by the Lord (2 Thess. 1:8-9).
C. Those who obey will be saved (Heb. 5:9).
D. Are you obedient unto God?

Conclusion

1. Do you have the proper regard for God?
2. Show your regard for God by obeying Him now.

Sacred Trusts

Introduction

1. Text: 1 Thessalonians 2:4
2. God has entrusted men with various things.

Discussion

I. The Gospel of Jesus Christ.

A. 1 Thessalonians 2:4; 1 Timothy 1:11-12
B. Acts 9, 22, 26 (Saul).
C. 1 Corinthians 9:16
D. Song: "Into Our Hands the Gospel Is Given."
E. Must be taught (2 Tim. 2:2).

II. Our Talents.

A. Matthew 25:14-30
B. Galatians 6:10
C. Ability + opportunity = responsibility!

III. Elders Watching for Souls.

A. Hebrews 13:17
B. Acts 20:28; 1 Peter 5:1-2
C. Luke 15:4-7 – Lost sheep
D. Elder's work involves souls.

IV. Our Children.

A. Psalm 127:3
B. Ephesians 6:4; Proverbs 22:6
C. As sacred trusts, we must love them and discipline them (Prov. 19:18; 29:15, 17).

V. Our Substance.

A. Proverbs 12:27; 3:9
B. Psalm 24:1

C. Important that we use it properly (Acts 5:1-11; 1 Cor. 16:1-2).

VI. Our Soul.

A. Matthew 16:26

B. 2 Corinthians 5:1

C. 1 Corinthians 6:19-20

D. 1 Peter 1:22; 3:1-4

E. It's the most valuable thing a man has!

VII. Time.

A. Psalm 90:12

B. Ephesians 5:16

C. Important to make the best use of the time that God gives us.

D. We all have the same amount of time!

VIII. Marriage.

A. Marriage is for life and it is a sacred trust that God holds man to.

B. Romans 7:1-4

C. Matthew 19:9

D. As husbands and wives, we must be faithful to discharge each and every responsibility.

Conclusion

1. How well are you doing with that which God has entrusted you?
2. What are you doing about your soul?

The Population of Hell

Introduction

1. Too little concern about hell.
2. A real place with real people being banished there (Luke 16). Majority will be there (Matt. 7:13-14).
3. Who will make up the population of hell?

Discussion

I. The Devil and His Angels.
   A. Matthew 25:41
   B. Revelation 20:10
   C. Hell is a prepared place!

II. People Who Satisfy the Lusts of the Flesh.
   A. Galatians 5:19-20
   B. 1 Corinthians 6:9
   C. Sin is serious (Rom. 6:23; Isa. 59:1-2).
   D. Must control (1 Cor. 9:27).

III. People Not in the Lord's Body.
   A. Ephesians 5:23-26
   B. 1 Corinthians 15:24; Colossians 1:18 – kingdom, body, and church one and the same.
   C. The saved are the body of Christ (Acts 2:47).
   D. Salvation is in Christ (2 Tim. 2:10).
   E. Galatians 3:27; Romans 6:3

IV. Religious People.
   A. Not all religious, sincere people will be saved.
   B. Matthew 7:21-23
   C. A person can be sincerely wrong (Acts 26:9; 22:16).
   D. Must study to know the truth (2 Tim. 2:15; John 8:32).

V. Good Moral People.

A. People argue that a good moral person can't be lost.

B. Acts 10:1-2, 22; 11:14 – Cornelius

C. Only Christ saves! If we can be saved by morality then we can save ourselves without Jesus!

VI. Lukewarm Church Members.

A. It's not enough to be baptized into the right church.

B. Revelation 3:15-16

C. We must be faithful (Rev. 2:10; 1 Cor. 15:58).

D. Some won't attend, worship, give, teach, study, pray, get involved and still think their going to Heaven.

E. James 2:14-26 – Must practice faith and works!

VII. People Refusing to Do Good Works.

A. Matthew 25:41-46

B. Remember Dorcas and the good works ". . . which she did" (Acts 10:36).

VIII. People Who Don't Know God or Disobey Him.

A. 2 Thessalonians 1:7-9

B. Some are atheists and many don't believe in the personal God of the Bible.

C. Must believe in Him (Heb. 11:6).

D. Gospel is God's power to save (Rom. 1:16).

E. Revelation 22:14; Hebrews 5:9

F. Discuss what obedience involves – HBRCB

IX. People Whose Names Are Not Written in the Book of Life.

A. Revelation 20:15

B. This is God's roll of the faithful.

C. Names written in when we obey, but can be blotted out (Rev. 3:5).

D. More important than "Who's Who."

Conclusion

1. Hell a terrible place of punishment (2 Thess. 1:9).
2. Can avoid by obeying (1 Cor. 6:9-11).

Three Things That Caused Felix to Tremble

Introduction

1. Text: Acts 24:24-25
2. The prophecy of Agabus (Acts 21:11) is soon fulfilled and Paul finds himself being arrested and on trial before the Sanhedrin. Later, Paul, upon a conspiracy to kill him, is removed to Caesarea. At Caesarea, Paul has three opportunities to present his defense and to preach the gospel of Christ to the Roman authorities who now hold him under arrest. Paul will appear before Felix, Festus, and Agrippa.
3. In this lesson, we are concerned about Paul's appearance before Felix, the governor and procurator of Judea.
4. Felix, having knowledge of these Christians, deferred Paul's first hearing (Acts 24:22). Then after certain days, he sent for Paul and heard him concerning the faith in Christ (Acts 24:24) and listened to the point that he "trembled." What was it that Paul said that caused Felix to tremble?

Discussion

I. Righteousness.

A. "Righteousness" refers to the qualities of being righteous or just.
B. The Bible regards the righteous!
C. We must awake to righteousness (1 Cor. 15:34).
D. We must put on the breastplate of righteousness (Eph. 6:14).
E. Follow after it (1 Tim. 6:11; 2 Tim. 2:22).
F. Paul spoke of a crown of righteousness (2 Tim. 4:8).
G. Some do righteousness (1 John 2:29; 3:7).
H. The righteousness of God is revealed in the gospel of Christ (Rom. 1:16-17).

II. Temperance.

A. "Temperance" refers to self-control and is to control or master the passions and desires of the body.
B. This matter was something the governor and his adulterous wife needed to hear!
C. Temperance is a fruit of the Spirit (Gal. 5:23).
D. As Peter discusses growth in Christ, he says, "add temperance" (2 Pet. 1:5-9).
E. To run in the race of life, one must be temperate. "Every man that striveth for the mastery is temperate in all things. . ." (1 Cor. 9:25).

III. Judgment to Come.

A. This is the anticipation of the final judgment that John saw in Revelation 20, when he saw the dead, small and great, stand before God (Rev. 20:12).
B. There will be a "day of judgment" (Matt. 12:26; Acts 17:31).
C. The time of the judgment is unknown (Mark 13:32).
D. The Father has committed all judgment to His Son (John 5:22).
E. All must appear before the judgment seat (2 Cor. 5:10).
F. The Lord will take vengeance on them that know not God, and that obey not the gospel (2 Thess. 1:7).
G. After death comes the judgment (Heb. 9:27).
H. The heavens and earth are kept in store unto the day of judgment (2 Pet. 3:7).
I. Man must prepare for the judgment to come or else incur the wrath of God!

Conclusion

1. Felix, after hearing about faith in Christ, said, "Go thy way for this time; when I have a convenient season, I will call for thee" (Acts 24:25). Some quiet their alarm by convincing themselves that they will pay attention later. As far as the record is concerned, Felix never did obey the gospel of Christ.
2. Don't be like Felix! Be like the Philippian Jailor who asked, "what must I do to be saved?" and responded in obedience to the Lord's will the "same hour of the night" (Acts 16:33).

"A Willing Heart"

Introduction

1. God has always required a willing heart (Exod. 35:4-5, 21-22).
2. To act willingly is to act voluntarily, gladly, cheerfully, and ungrudgingly.
3. Here are some areas in which we need to be willing.

Discussion

I. Willing to Serve.

A. 1 Chronicles 28:9
B. The Lord requires that we serve Him with a willing heart (Deut. 10:12).
C. We are to serve God acceptably with reverence and godly fear (Heb. 12:28).
D. The Father honors those who serve (John 12:26).
E. A reward is in store for those who serve the Lord faithfully (Col. 3:24).
F. We should be willing to serve one another (Gal. 5:13).

II. Willing to Teach.

A. 2 Timothy 2:2
B. 2 Timothy 2:24
C. Matthew 28:19-20
D. John 6:44-45
E. Older women to teach the younger women (Tit. 2:4).
F. Parents to teach children (Deut. 6:7-9; Eph. 6:4).

III. Willing to Work.

A. Nehemiah 4:6
B. The virtuous woman worked willingly with her hands (Prov. 31:13).
C. We are taught to work with our hands (Eph. 4:28; 1 Thess. 4:11; 2 Thess. 3:10).
D. Jesus had a mind to work (John 4:34; 9:4).
E. We should always abound in the work of the Lord (1 Cor. 15:58).

IV. Willing to Pray.

A. 1 Thessalonians 5:17
B. Jesus prayed willingly (John 14:16).
C. The Lord taught that we ought always to pray (Luke 18:1).
D. We must be instant or faithful in prayer (Rom. 12:12).

V. Willing to Study.

A. Acts 17:11
B. 2 Timothy 2:15
C. Bible study has great benefits:
   1. Builds up (Acts 20:32).
   2. Makes one wise unto salvation (2 Tim. 3:15-16).
D. Are you willing to put forth the effort to study?

VI. Willing to Sing.

A. 1 Corinthians 14:15
B. Ephesians 5:19
C. Singing is a means of teaching and admonishing one another (Col. 3:16).
D. We praise God through singing (Heb. 2:12).

VII. Willing to Give.

A. God has always demanded that His people give willingly!
   1. The offering for the tabernacle (Exod. 25:2).
   2. The offering for the temple (1 Chron. 29:6).
   3. The offering for the Passover (2 Chron. 35:8).
B. The brethren of Macedonia gave willingly (2 Cor. 8:3-5).
C. We ought to give with a willing heart (2 Cor. 9:7).

VIII. Willing to Obey.

A. Romans 6:16-18
B. We ought to obey God (Acts 5:29).
C. Salvation belongs to the obedient (Heb. 5:9).
D. Those who do not obey will be punished (2 Thess. 1:8-9).

Conclusion

1. Do you have a willing heart?
2. Are you willing to come today in obedience to the Lord?

Playing the Fool

Introduction

1. Text: 1 Samuel 26:21
2. Relate the story of David and Saul.
3. A number are said to play the fool.

Discussion

I. When One Says There Is No God.

A. Psalm 14:1

B. The reason that one is playing the fool when he says there is no God is because there is a God!

1. Genesis 1:1
2. Psalm 19:1
3. Psalm 90:1-2
4. Acts 17:28

C. Some say, "I have never seen God and I don't believe in anything I can't see." I ask, "Have you ever seen your brain?"

II. When a Way Is Right by One's Own Standard.

A. Proverbs 12:15

B. Proverbs 28:26

C. Why is this so?

1. Jeremiah 10:23
2. Isaiah 55:8-9

D. The downfall of Israel began when "every man did that which was right in his own eyes" (Judg. 21:25).

E. When folks say, "I thought" (2 Kings 5:11) or "it seems to me."

F. We need to ask, "for what saith the Scripture?" (Rom. 4:3) or "Speak Lord, thy servant heareth" (1 Sam. 3:10). We need to say, as did Cornelius, "We are present before God to hear all things that are commanded . . . of God" (Acts 10:33).

G. A person may "fly by the seat of his pants" but play the fool when he tries to please God that way!

III. Those Who Mock at Sin.

A. Proverbs 14:9

B. Attitude toward sin is not what it once was. Some today even poke fun at sin.

C. Sin does what it has always done (Isa. 59:1-2; Rom. 6:23; Jas. 1:14-15).

D. A lot of folks have given sin a good white-washing, but it still leads to "being cast into outer darkness" (Matt. 25:30).

IV. Those Who Leave God Out of Their Plans.

A. Luke 12:20

B. James 4:13-16

C. What's all this about? Read and study the story in Luke 12:15-21.

1. He was selfish (Notice "I" and "my").
2. He was not rich toward God (Luke 12:21).

V. Unfaithful Church Members.

A. Galatians 3:1

B. Galatians 5:7

C. Hindered by Satan (1 Thess. 2:18).

1. Ephesians 4:27
2. 2 Corinthians 2:11
3. 1 Peter 5:8
4. 2 Corinthians 11:2

VI. Those Who Do Not Prepare to Meet God.

A. Matthew 25:1-12

1. The wise and foolish virgins.
2. Note the difference in the two groups.
3. Note Matthew 25:10

B. Matthew 7:21-27

1. Contrast the two builders.
2. One prepared and one not.

Conclusion

Is it possible that you have been "playing the fool"?

Liberalism: I Believe in It!

Introduction

1. Word "liberal" means "generous; not stingy."
2. While we must be conservative in regards to respecting Bible authority (Gal. 1:8-9; 2 John 9-11; Rev. 22:18-19), there are some areas in which we must be liberal.

Discussion

I. Hospitality.

A. Romans 12:13
B. 1 Peter 4:9
C. "Love of strangers."
D. Hebrews 13:2
E. Deacons and elders (1 Tim. 3:2; Tit. 1:8).

II. Giving.

A. Romans 12:8 – "simplicity" (liberality).
B. 2 Corinthians 9:6
C. Remember widow's mite (Mark 12).
D. Israel's liberality was seen in that they gave about 1/3.
E. 2 Corinthians 8:9

III. Kindness.

A. Ephesians 4:32
B. 2 Peter 1:7
C. Galatians 5:22-23 – Fruit of Spirit
D. 1 Corinthians 13:4
E. Kindness is goodness of heart in action.
F. Good Samaritan (Luke 10).

IV. Forgiveness.

A. Ephesians 4:32
B. Matthew 6:14-15

C. Matthew 18:21-22, 35
D. Mark 11:25 – Must forgive if we expect forgiveness.

V. Benevolence.

A. Galatians 6:10
B. James 1:27
C. 1 John 3:17
D. 1 Timothy 6:18
E. Matthew 25:35-36
F. 2 Corinthians 8-9
G. A difference between individual and church responsibility (1 Tim. 5:16).

Conclusion

1. How liberal are we when it comes to these things?
2. Don't you believe in liberalism?

An Ancient Father's Admonition to His Son

Introduction

1. Have you ever wondered how a father, who lived over 3,000 years ago, might have admonished his son?
2. Text: 1 Chronicles 28:9
3. In this text, we have David, as king of Israel, giving admonition to his son, Solomon, who will soon take over the leadership of the Israelite nation.
4. Let's notice what this ancient father had to say to his son.

Discussion

I. Know God.

A. "Know" means to have understanding of.

B. Too many people are like the Gentiles who refused to know God (Rom. 1:21). Further, ". . . they did not like to retain God in their knowledge" (Rom. 1:28).

C. Paul knew God (2 Tim. 1:12).

D. How can we know God? (1 John 2:3-4).

E. What fathers should tell their sons about God:

1. He is Creator (Ps. 14:1; Gen. 1:27).
2. He is Almighty (Rev. 4:8).
3. He is Judge (Eccl. 11:9).
4. He is Saviour (1 Tim. 4:10; Hosea 13:4).

F. Paul spoke of those who "profess" they know God (Tit. 1:16).

II. Serve God.

A. To serve God means to give respect and obedience to God. Service to God has always been required.

B. This father told his son *how* to serve God. With a perfect heart and with a willing mind (2 Cor. 8:12).

C. Ours is to be a whole-hearted service to God! (Mark 12:30).
D. Matthew 6:24
E. We must serve God "acceptably with reverence and godly fear" (Heb. 12:28).

III. Remember That the Lord Searches All Hearts.

A. This ancient father calls upon his son to remember that the Lord searches all hearts and understands all imaginations of the thoughts.
B. This statement reminds us of the one made to Samuel when David was being selected King (1 Sam. 16:7).
C. David spoke of how God searched and knew him (Ps. 139:13). In Psalm 139:23-24, David welcomed God's search of him.
D. God knew the evil imaginations of the hearts of men in the days of Noah (Gen. 6:5).
E. Our thoughts can defile us (Matt. 15:19-20).
F. We shall give account for our thoughts and actions, even every idle word (Matt. 12:36).

IV. Seek the Lord.

A. The father's promise is that if he will seek the Lord, "he will be found of thee."
B. This seeking has to do with making an effort to find something. In this case, it is the Lord.
C. Jeremiah 29:13
D. Some sought the Lord for the wrong reason and were rebuked of the Lord (John 6:26).
E. Notice what Paul told the Athenians (Acts 17:27).
F. Eternal life is promised to those who seek glory, honor, and immortality (Rom. 2:7).
G. What are you seeking? Some are seeking wealth, pleasure, power, etc. Seek the Lord!

V. If You Forsake the Lord He Will Cast Thee Off Forever.

A. It is a serious thing to forsake the Lord!
B. "Forsake" suggests "to give up, renounce, or leave." Once you have sought the Lord and found Him, don't leave Him or renounce Him!
C. Joshua 24:20
D. If we do the will of the Lord, He has promised, ". . . I will never leave thee, nor forsake thee" (Heb. 13:5).
E. Man is the one who does the forsaking, not God! We forsake God when we turn aside and do that which is evil in His sight. If we forsake the Lord, He turns aside by casting us off forever! Think about being cast off forever!

Conclusion

1. Would this be the kind of thing you would tell your son? (Eph. 6:4).
2. May we all take advantage of these wise words and apply them to our lives.

"Who Is A Wise Man?"

Introduction

1. James 3:13
2. There are basically two categories of people: wise and foolish.
3. In this study, we are concerned with who is a wise man.

Discussion

I. The Man Who Refrains His Lips.

A. Proverbs 10:19
B. Proverbs 17:28
C. Proverbs 29:11
D. A man's failure to refrain his lips renders his religion vain (Jas. 1:26).
E. Refraining our lips will help keep us from sinning with the tongue (Ps. 39:1).

II. The Man Who Wins Souls.

A. Proverbs 11:30
B. This implies that men have souls (Gen. 2:7; Zech. 12:1).
C. The soul is man's most valuable possession (Matt. 16:26).
D. Winning souls is teaching others and bringing them to Jesus (2 Tim. 2:2; John 1:40-42).
E. Are you a soul winner?

III. The Man Who Hears His Father's Instruction.

A. Proverbs 13:1
B. Proverbs 4:1
C. Some fail to heed a father's instruction and such makes one foolish.
D. Children are to obey their parents (Eph. 6:1; Col. 3:20).

IV. The Man Who Hears and Obeys.

A. Matthew 7:24-27
B. We must be doers of the word and not hearers only (Rom. 2:13; Jas. 1:22-

25).
C. How are you building, spiritually?

V. The Man Who Makes Preparation.
A. Matthew 25:1-13
B. Christ will come unexpectedly (2 Pet. 3:10).
C. We must be prepared for His coming (Matt. 24:42-44).
D. Are you prepared?

VI. The Man Who Redeems the Time.
A. Ephesians 5:15-16
B. Colossians 4:5
C. To redeem the time is to buy up each opportunity.
D. We must make good use of the time God has given us (Ps. 90:12; 2 Cor. 6:2).

VII. The Man Who Knows the Scriptures.
A. 2 Timothy 3:15
B. Wisdom comes from knowing the Scriptures!
C. Knowledge of the Scriptures comes by reading and diligent study (Eph. 3:4; 2 Tim. 2:15).
D. Do you know the Scriptures?

VIII. The Man Who Shows His Works.
A. James 3:13
B. Works are not of any value unless they are demonstrated (Jas. 2:14-26).
C. These are not works about which we boast (Eph. 2:9).

Conclusion
1. Are you a wise man?
2. Show your works in obeying the gospel now, and be wise!

Pleasing God

Introduction

1. Our most important thought must be that of pleasing God.
2. Hebrews 11:5; Genesis 5:24
3. Let's notice some things which pleased God.

Discussion

I. The Death of Christ.

A. Isaiah 53:10
B. Hebrews 9:22
C. Hebrews 10:4
D. Hebrews 10:9-13, 17
E. The death of Jesus satisfied the demands of God.

II. Foolishness of Preaching.

A. 1 Corinthians 1:21
B. Preaching has been God's way of teaching men His truths.
   1. 1 Peter 1:11
   2. 1 Peter 3:18-20
   3. Mark 16:15
   4. Titus 1:3
C. Contrast foolish preaching with the "foolishness of preaching."
   1. 1 Corinthians 1:18-21
   2. Galatians 4:4-5

III. When Children Obey Their Parents.

A. God has always expected children to be obedient to their parents.
   1. Ephesians 6:1-2
   2. Colossians 3:20
B. Provisions made for teaching and punishment.
   1. Deuteronomy 6:6-9

2. Deuteronomy 21:18-21

C. Today, child correction, even in the mildest form, is almost unheard of!

D. We will live to see the consequences of an uncorrected society!

IV. In Preaching the Gospel.

A. 1 Thessalonians 2:4

B. Galatians 1:8-9

C. A young man was told, "You can't preach the gospel as strong in the south as you can in the north!" Did you ever read anything in the Word of God like that?

D. 2 Timothy 4:1-4

E. Galatians 1:10

V. The Life of Christ.

A. Matthew 3:17

B. Matthew 17:5

C. Discuss His life:

1. Perfect (1 Pet. 2:21; 2 Cor. 5:21).
2. Obedient (Heb. 5:8-9).

VI. Praising God in Singing.

A. Psalm 69:30-31

B. Everyone is commanded to sing (Eph. 5:19; Col. 3:16; Heb. 2:12).

C. Whatever I am told to do in making music to the Lord, you are told to do!

VII. The Resurrected New Body.

A. 1 Corinthians 15:25-28

B. Philippians 3:21; 1 John 3:2

C. We may not know what the new spiritual body will look like, but we do know that it will please God.

Conclusion

Have you done the things which please God?

Young Christians and Their Parents

Introduction

1. Young people have responsibilities in the home.
2. Parent-child relationship a problem today.
3. Let's notice some obligations of young people to their parents.

Discussion

I. Heed Their Instruction.

A. Proverbs 1:7-8

B. Some kids think they know everything and dismiss parental advice as out of date.

C. Godly parents have their children's interest first.

D. Mark Twain said, "When I was a boy of 14, my father was so ignorant I could hardly stand to have the old man around. But when I had got to be 21, I was astonished at how much he had learned in 7 years."

II. Obey Them.

A. Deuteronomy 21:18-21

B. Ephesians 6:1; Colossians 3:20

C. Must submit to their authority and not be rebellious.

D. Jesus obeyed (Luke 2:51).

E. Remember the context of ". . .disobedient to parents. . ." (Rom. 1:30).

F. Serious sin to disobey!

III. Don't Despise Their Discipline.

A. None particularly like discipline, but it's for one's own good. Discipline suggests training.

B. Parents are required to discipline their children (Prov. 22:6; 19:18).

C. Hebrews 12:7 – discipline teaches respect.

IV. Honor Them.

A. Ephesians 6:2-3
B. Greatly needed by young people today. .
C. More than obedience, proper attitude.
D. Honor in action (even when one disagrees).
    1. Obey – listen to their advice.
    2. Recognize they are human.
    3. Treat them right.
    4. Be kind to them.
    5. Speak respectfully to them.
    6. Help them.
    7. Show appreciation to them.
    8. Don't blame failure on them.

V. Care for Them When Needed.

A. 1 Timothy 5:4, 16 – "requite" (repay).
B. They took care of us!
C. May come a time when they will need your help.

VI. Obey God First.

A. Children owe God and their parents this responsibility.
B. Acts 5:29
C. Matthew 10:37
D. Children have responsibility to God and God will hold them accountable (Eccl. 12:13-14).
E. Can't go to Heaven on parent's coattails!

Conclusion

1. Each of us have individual responsibility.
2. As a young person, do your part and fulfill your obligations to your parents!

Bible Ought's

Introduction

1. Text: Genesis 34:7
2. God's Word tells a man what he ought and ought not do.
3. Let's notice some Bible ought's.

Discussion

I. We Ought to Obey God.

A. Acts 5:29

B. When Peter and the apostles were told to not preach in the Lord's name, they responded by saying, "We ought to obey God rather than men."

C. This is a good attitude that needs to be cultivated among God's people today.

D. God must be obeyed (Rom. 6:17; 1 John 5:2-3).

II. Men Ought Always to Pray.

A. Luke 18:1

B. ". . . We know not what we should pray for as we ought. . ." (Rom. 8:26).

C. "Pray without ceasing" (1 Thess. 5:17).

D. "Praying always with all prayer and supplication. . ." (Eph. 6:18).

E. Prayer should be a regular part of our lives.

III. Men Ought to Love Their Wives.

A. Ephesians 5:28

B. A man ought to love his wife as himself (Eph. 5:28-30) and as Christ loved the church (Eph. 5:25).

C. This love is the disposition of the heart that seeks her very best.

D. Notice love's qualities (1 Cor. 13:4-8).

IV. We Ought to Give the More Earnest Heed.

A. Hebrews 2:1

B. We need to pay strict attention to God's Word!

C. The Bible puts emphasis on being a hearer and a doer (Rom. 2:13; Jas.

1:22-25).

D. Otherwise, these things may "slip" (lose the benefit of these things).

E. The Word is able to build up and give an inheritance (Acts 20:32).

V. We Ought to Love One Another.

A. 1 John 4:11

B. God loved us enough to send His own Son (1 John 4:9-10).

C. Loving God requires loving your brother (1 John 4:20-21).

D. Love with a pure heart fervently (1 Pet. 1:22).

Conclusion

1. Those who do as they "ought," ought to understand their responsibility to obey.
2. Peter told Cornelius what he ought to do (Acts 10:6). He heard the Word, believed it, and obeyed it through baptism (Acts 10:44-48).
3. Won't you come and do that which you ought?

Worshipping God in Spirit

Introduction

1. There are two elements of acceptable worship: spirit and truth (John 4:24).
2. The Bible places emphasis upon worshipping God in spirit (Matt. 15:8; Phil. 3:3; Col. 3:23).
3. Here is how we worship God in spirit.

Discussion

I. Pray with Spirit.

A. 1 Corinthians 14:15
B. Ephesians 6:18
C. Prayer is our way of talking to God (Phil. 4:6).
D. We need to put our hearts into our prayers! We must be honest and sincere in what we say.
E. We must not pray to be seen of men (Matt. 6:5).
F. We must not use vain repetitions (Matt. 6:7).
G. Does your prayer come from the heart?

II. Sing with Spirit.

A. 1 Corinthians 14:15
B. Ephesians 5:19
C. We are to sing with all of our heart, soul, and mind!
D. Singing is a means of praising God (Heb. 2:12) and teaching and admonishing one another (Col. 3:16).
E. We need to meditate on the words that we are singing.
F. Do you put your heart into your singing?

III. Observe the Lord's Supper with Spirit.

A. 1 Corinthians 11:23-29
B. The Lord's supper was instituted by Christ and is observed by Christians.
C. It is observed on the first day of the week (Acts 20:7).
D. We are to discern the Lord's body!

E. When you observe the Lord's supper is your mind centered around the death of Christ?

IV. Give with Spirit.

A. God has always required His people to give from the heart (Exod. 25:2).
B. We are commanded to give to support the work of the church (1 Cor. 16:1-2).
C. We ought to give cheerfully (2 Cor. 9:7).
D. Do you give because you want to or because you have to?

V. Teach with Spirit.

A. Acts 20:7
B. 2 Timothy 2:2
C. Teaching plays an important role in converting folks to the Lord (Matt. 28:19-20; John 6:44-45).
D. We need to put some enthusiasm in our teaching (Ezek. 6:11; Acts 8:30).
E. What we say needs to come from the heart!
F. Do you teach with spirit?

Conclusion

1. If we leave spirit out of our worship, our worship is vain! (Matt. 15:8-9).
2. Obey God now and serve Him with all of your being.

What I Was and What I Am

Introduction

1. There are some in our society who do not know who they are. They have to go out and "find themselves."
2. 1 Corinthians 15:10; 1 Timothy 1:12-16

Discussion

I. Dead But Now Alive.

   A. Death is a separation. When one is in sin, he is said to be dead (Eph. 2:1). "To quicken" is "to make alive."
   B. Colossians 2:13
   C. Romans 6:6-8

II. Old Man Now a New Man.

   A. Colossians 3:9-10
   B. Romans 6:1-6
   C. Acts 2:38
   D. Died, buried, raised in baptism (Rom. 6:16-18).

III. Alienated Now Reconciled

   A. Colossians 1:11
   B. Ephesians 2:16
      1. By the cross.
      2. In one body, the church (Col. 1:24).
      3. No way one can be brought into proper relationship with God without Christ, the cross, and the church!

IV. Far Off Now Nigh.

   A. Ephesians 2:13
      1. Discuss the former state of these Ephesian Christians (Eph. 2:11-12).
      2. Notice how their change took place (Acts 19:1-6).
   B. Notice the part the blood of Christ played.
      1. Ephesians 2:13

2. Revelation 1:5

V. Strangers and Foreigners Now Fellowcitizens.

A. Ephesians 2:19

B. Discuss Ephesians 2:19-22.

1. Strangers
2. Foreigners
3. Fellowcitizens

C. What a contrast!

VI. In the World Now Translated into the Kingdom.

A. Ephesians 2:12

B. Colossians 1:13

1. Yet some say the kingdom has not been established.
2. It has been established (Rev. 1:9).
3. Will be delivered up to God at the end of time, not set up (1 Cor. 15:23-24).

Conclusion

1. Now take a look at yourself as to what you are right now and what you can become, even right now.
2. If you need to make some changes in your life, come at this time, believing, and obeying.

The Prodigal Son

Introduction

1. Jesus often used parables in His teaching.
2. Parables illustrate the truth and cause people to relate to and understand what's being taught.
3. Parables are stories concerning every day life with spiritual meaning.
4. Let's study one such parable and learn some valuable lessons. Text: Luke 15:11-24.

Discussion

I. Lessons about God.

A. God Is Good.
   1. Father represents God and son made no complaint against father.
   2. Father gave son inheritance (Luke 15:12).
   3. Treated servants well (Luke 15:17).

B. God Does Not Force Us to Serve Him.
   1. He let son go (Luke 15:12).
   2. Did not force son to come home (Luke 15:20).
   3. God created man as a free moral agent.

C. God Is Compassionate and Forgiving.
   1. May have been looking for son's return (Luke 15:20).
   2. Gave ring, robe, shoes, etc. – Forgave and restored sonship (Luke 15:22-23).
   3. God is always ready to forgive.

II. Lessons from Mistakes of the Son.

A. Sin Is a Choice We Make.
   1. Son chose to leave (Luke 15:12).
   2. Admitted later, "I have sinned" (Luke 15:18).
   3. We are responsible for the choices we make.

B. Sin Is a Journey Away from God.

1. Left home and took journey into far country (Luke 15:13).
2. There he lived riotously (Luke 15:13).
3. Sin brings separation (Isa. 59:1-2; Luke 15:24).

C. Riotous Living Is a Waste.
1. He wasted his substance with such living (Luke 15:13).
2. "Prodigal" means wasteful.
3. He gathered all together only to scatter it abroad (Luke 15:13).
4. He wasted his money, time, energies, and opportunities.
5. Sin is a perversion of good and this son ended up with nothing.

D. We Reap What We Sow.
1. Unchangeable law.
2. Galatians 6:7
3. Look at what he reaped. Money was gone, was in want, feeding swine, starving, no one would give to him, etc (Luke 15:14-16). A pathetic picture!
4. Sin has its consequences (Prov. 13:15).

III. Lessons from Son's Virtues.

A. We Need to Come to Ourselves.
1. Son finally came to his senses (Luke 15:17).
2. Began to see himself for what he had become.
3. We need to recognize what sin does for us.
4. When he came to himself, it brought about conviction of sin, but also resolution to change.
5. Many never come to themselves.

B. The Necessity of Action.
1. He acted on his resolution (Luke 15:20).
2. Showed initiative.
3. Easy to see need for change, but hard to actually change.
4. "Road to hell is paved with good intentions."

C. Recognize God's Blessings Are Available.
1. He knew the right place to go.
2. He knew father had much to offer (Luke 15:17).
3. Only true joy and satisfaction through God.

D. We Must Accept Full Blame for Our Sins.
1. ". . . I have sinned . . ." (Luke 15:18).
2. Could blame no one else.
3. Made no excuses for his actions.

E. The Need for Humble Penitence.
1. Had to put pride aside to accept blame for sin and return.
2. Hard to say, "I have sinned."
3. Wanted to be just a humble servant (Luke 15:19).
4. He was not arrogant over his sin. He recognized that he deserved noth-

ing and that anything he would receive would be by the father's grace.

5. Some are never truly penitent.

F. The Blessing of Confession.
   1. Went back and confessed wrong (Luke 15:21).
   2. Blessing and forgiveness followed his confession (Luke 15:22-24).
   3. Forgiven only after he came out of sin, repented, and confessed.
   4. James 5:16

Conclusion

1. Won't you leave your riotous living, come to your senses, and come to a loving God?
2. Walk down that road now!

Bible Ought Not's

Introduction

1. Text: Genesis 34:7
2. God's Word tells a man what he ought and ought not do.
3. Let's notice some Bible ought not's.

Discussion

I. Ought Not to Think That the Godhead Is Like unto Gold.

A. Acts 17:29

B. Paul was speaking to the Athenians concerning the "unknown God" (Acts 17:22-25, 28).

C. The Godhead (Deity) is not like unto gold, silver, or stone!

D. The Godhead has attributes of personality:

1. The Father loves (John 3:16).
2. The Father has life in Himself (John 5:26).
3. The Son can speak (John 6:63).
4. The Son has knowledge (John 10:14).
5. The Holy Spirit speaks (1 Tim. 4:1).
6. The Holy Spirit guides (John 16:13).

E. The Psalmist spoke of the characteristics of idols (Ps. 115:4-8).

F. In God ". . . we live and move and have our being" (Acts 17:28).

II. Man Ought Not to Think Too Highly of Himself.

A. Romans 12:3

B. To think soberly is to think sensibly – to think of our proper relations with God and our fellowman.

C. God's people must be humble (Col. 3:12; 1 Pet. 5:5).

III. Blessings and Cursings Out of the Same Mouth Ought Not So to Be.

A. James 3:10

B. James is speaking of the tongue (Jas. 3:5-6, 8-12).

C. It is inconsistent and sinful for man's mouth to utter praise to God, and then to curse men made in God's likeness.

D. Man will give account for every word (Matt. 12:36-37).

E. Proverbs 15:1-2

IV. Some Things Ought Not to Be Spoken or Taught.

A. Paul spoke of tattlers who go from house to house and speak things they ought not (1 Tim. 5:13).

B. He also spoke of false teachers who subvert whole houses, teaching things which they ought not (Tit. 1:11).

C. These folks stand in need of a good rebuking (Tit. 1:13).

D. Notice what the end will be of false teachers (1 Pet. 2:1-9).

Conclusion

1. While some things ought not to be done, other things ought to be done.
2. Won't you come and do that which you ought?

Baptism as Taught in the Epistles

Introduction

1. The Bible has a lot to say about baptism.
2. In this study, we are concerned about baptism as it is taught in the epistles.

Discussion

I. Baptism Is One.

A. Ephesians 4:4-6

B. The Bible mentions several baptisms (Heb. 6:2).

1 Baptism of Moses (1 Cor. 10:1-11).

2. Baptism of suffering (Matt. 20:20-23).

3 Baptism of John (Matt. 3:1-6).

4. Baptism of the Holy Spirit (Matt. 3:11).

5 Baptism of fire (Matt. 3:11-12).

C. When Paul wrote the Ephesians, there was one baptism – the baptism of the great commission (Mark 16:15-16).

II. Baptism Puts One into Christ.

A. Galatians 3:26-28

B. Some things found in Christ.

1. Salvation (2 Tim. 2:10).
2. Spiritual blessings (Eph. 1:3).
3. Redemption (Rom. 3:24).
4. Sanctification (1 Cor. 1:2).
5. Liberty (Gal. 2:4).
6. Reconciliation (Eph. 2:13).
7. Promise of life (2 Tim. 1:1).

C. Are you in Christ?

III. Baptism Puts One into the One Body.

A. 1 Corinthians 12:13
B. The body is the church (Col. 1:24).
C. The saved are added to the church (Acts 2:47).
D. One cannot be a member of the church without being baptized the Bible way.

IV. Baptism Is a Burial.

A. Colossians 2:11-13
B. Romans 6:3-4
C. Baptism is not a sprinkling or a pouring!
D. The element one is buried in is water (Acts 8:36-38).

V. Baptism Is a Planting.

A. Romans 6:5
B. When one plants a seed in the ground, he doesn't sprinkle a little dirt over it – he completely covers it.
C. Have you been planted?

VI. Baptism Is in the Name of Christ.

A. 1 Corinthians 1:11-17
B. Paul was thankful that he baptized no more than he did because they were saying that he baptized in his own name.
C. Matthew 28:19-20
D. Acts 10:48
E. Have you been baptized in the name of Christ?

VII. Baptism Saves.

A. 1 Peter 3:21
B. Baptism is important because salvation is its result.
C. Mark 16:16
D. Acts 2:38
E. Acts 22:16

Conclusion

1. The epistles say a lot about baptism.
2. We urge you to be baptized the Bible way.

The Shortest Funeral Sermon

Introduction

1. Funerals are as old as man himself.
2. God preached the funeral sermon of Moses in five words (Josh. 1:1-2).

Discussion

I. "Moses."

- A. Discuss some facts about Moses:
  - 1 The child (Exod. 12).
  - 2. He was very great (Exod. 11:3).
  - 3. He was meek (Num. 12:3).
  - 4. Lawgiver (John 1:17).
  - 5 Man of God (Deut. 33:1).
  - 6. Faithful (Heb. 3:2, 5).
  - 7. Mentioned in the great faith chapter (Heb. 11:23-28).
- B. Could these things be said about you?

II. "My."

- A. He was God's.
- B. So should we be (1 Cor. 6:20).
- C. Do you belong to God?

III. "Servant."

- A. Exodus 14:31
- B. Deuteronomy 34:5
  - 1. To die a servant of God, you must be one while you live!
    - a. Romans 6:16
    - b. Romans 6:22
  - 2. Are you a servant of God?

IV. "Is."

- A. Moses, like all men, died.
  - 1. Deuteronomy 33:5-12

2. Ecclesiastes 9:5
3. Romans 5:12
4. 1 Corinthians 15:22
5. Hebrews 9:27

B. The only exception (1 Cor. 15:51-54).

V. "Dead."

A. Death is a separation.
B. Deuteronomy 34:5-6; Jude 9
C. James 2:26
D. Deuteronomy 34:8
E. Not as much sorrow when a child of God dies (1 Thess. 4:13).

Conclusion

1. Moses was 120 (Deut. 34:7).
2. Psalm 90:10-12
   a. Come and make your life what it ought to be with God as you can be ready for death.
   b. God's plan for us is to hear, believe, repent, confess our faith, be baptized, and then live "righteously, and godly" (Tit. 2:11-12).

The Death of David's Child

Introduction

1. Give background on David's sin with Bathsheba and Nathan's visit (2 Sam. 11).
2. Read 2 Samuel 12:15-23.
3. Lessons learned from story.

Discussion

I. Consequences of Sin.

A. Loss of child was result of David's sin.
B. Nathan told David of God's punishment (2 Sam. 12:13-14).
C. Some think they can sin with immunity!
D. Sin has consequences (Gal. 6:7; Num. 32:23).
E. Sin brings God's punishment (Rom. 6:23; Isa. 59:1-2).
F. Some consequences of sin remain after being forgiven. David admitted sin (2 Sam. 12:13), asked for forgiveness (Ps. 51:1-3), and still the child died.
G. Think seriously about what you do.

II. Children Are Safe.

A. 2 Samuel 12:23
B. If one dies in infancy he will go to Heaven.
C. Children are not born sinners.
D. Luke 18:16; Matthew 18:3
E. We are responsible for our own sin (1 John 3:4).
F. Ezekiel 18:19-20

III. There Is Life After Death.

A. 2 Samuel 12:23- ". . . I shall go to him. . . ."
B. Some scoff at idea of life after death.
C. Man has an eternal spirit (2 Cor. 5:1; Eccl. 12:7).
D. Luke 16:19-31 – picture of life after death.
E. We must prepare for life after death.

IV. No Reincarnation.

A. Some believe you come back to life in another form.
B. Boy could not return (2 Sam. 12:23).
C. Man only dies once (Heb. 9:27).

V. God Gives Us Strength.

A. There are many tragedies in life and God will help.
B. David's strength to go on and face life came from God (2 Sam. 12:20).
C. Some want to blame God rather than accept His help.
D. Psalm 121; 46:1-2; 23

VI. We Can Go to Heaven.

A. 2 Samuel 12:23 – ". . . go to him."
B. Heaven is a prepared place for a prepared people (John 14:2-3).
C. Revelation 21:1-7

Conclusion

1. Have we learned these lessons?
2. We too, can ". . . go to him . . ." (2 Sam. 12:23).

Obedience in the Fifth Book of Moses

Introduction

1. The book of Deuteronomy, the fifth book of Moses, consists of a series of farewell messages by Israel's 120-year-old leader, Moses. It is addressed to the new generation who will possess the promised land of Canaan – those who survived the forty years of wilderness wandering.
2. Moses is reminding the new generation of the importance of obedience and explains to them what obedience involves.

Discussion

I. Obedience Involved Doing God's Will.

A. Emphasis put on doing God's will!
B. Deuteronomy 4:1 – "for to do them. . . ."
C. Deuteronomy 4:5-6 – "Keep therefore and do them. . . ."
D. Deuteronomy 5:1 – "learn them, and keep, and do them."
E. Deuteronomy 6:3 – "Hear . . . and observe to do it. . . ."
F. Deuteronomy 6:17-18 – ". . . diligently keep the commandments. . . ."
G. Deuteronomy 6:24-25 – "commanded us to do all these statutes. . . ."
H. A blessing comes to those who obey (Deut. 11:27) and a curse to those who do not obey (Deut. 11:28).
I. Deuteronomy 27:9-10 – ". . . therefore obey. . . ."
J. Deuteronomy 28:1-2 – ". . . observe to do all his commandment. . . ."
K. The failure to obey brought consequences (Deut. 28:15).
L. Something to do under the law of Christ (Matt. 7:24-27; Heb. 5:9; Rev. 22:14).

II. Obedience Involved Not Tampering with God's Will.

A. Deuteronomy 4:2
B. Don't tamper with God's Word!

C. Deuteronomy 12:32
D. Final warning (Rev. 22:18-19).

III. Obedience Involved Teaching.

A. Deuteronomy 4:9
B. Why? (Deut. 4:10).
C. People have a tendency to forget (Deut. 4:23; 6:12; 8:11, 14).
D. Put God's Word in your heart so you can teach your children diligently (Deut. 6:7-10).
E. Your son might ask you a question (Deut. 6:20).
F. ". . . lay up my words in your heart. . ." (Deut. 11:18-21).
G. They were to read the law so they would observe to do and so their children may hear and fear (Deut. 31:11-13).
H. Moses spoke of "children in whom is no faith" (Deut. 32:20).
I. Ephesians 6:4
J. Obedience involves discipline in the home (Deut. 21:18-21; Prov. 22:6; 19:18).

IV. Obedience Involved Fear, Walking in His Way, Love, and Service.

A. Deuteronomy 10:12-13
B. This is what the Lord required of Israel. Does He require any less of His people today?
C. "Fear God" (1 Pet. 2:17).
D. Jesus is the way, the truth, and the life (John 14:6).
E. "Love the Lord thy God" (Matt. 22:37; John 14:15).
F. "Servants to God" (Rom. 6:22).

V. Obedience Involved Turning Away the False Prophet.

A. Deuteronomy 13:1-2 tells how to identify such.
B. Don't listen to the false prophet (Deut. 13:2-4).
C. What was to happen to that false prophet? (Deut. 13:5).
D. What about enticing one to go astray (Deut. 13:6-11).
E. 2 John was written to warn about false teachers (2 John 7-11).

VI. Obedience Involved Keeping the Passover.

A. Deuteronomy 16:16 – Keep the passover.
B. Instituted in memory of Israel's preservation from the last plague visited upon Egypt, the death of the firstborn.
C. Three times a year the males appeared before the Lord (Deut. 16:16).
D. Today, we keep the first day of the week and observe the Lord's supper, which was instituted when the Lord observed the Passover (Matt. 26:26-29).
E. Disciples came together and broke bread on the first day of the week (Acts 20:7).

VII. Obedience Involved Doing Nothing Presumptuously.

A. Deuteronomy 17:12-13
B. We can't presume a thing!
C. Peter spoke of the presumptuous in 2 Peter 2:10.
D. Remember Nadab and Abihu in Leviticus 10:1-2?

Conclusion

1. Our obedience is unto Jesus Christ (Heb. 5:8-9).
2. Won't you come in obedience today?

The One Body

Introduction

1. The Bible presents the one body (Eph. 4:4).
2. Let's notice some things the Bible teaches about the one body.

Discussion

I. The Body Is the Church.

A. Colossians 1:18
B. Colossians 1:24
C. Ephesians 1:22-23
D. Since there is one body, there is just one church.

II. The Body Is Headed by Christ.

A. Colossians 1:18
B. Ephesians 1:22-23
C. Ephesians 4:15
D. Ephesians 5:23
E. The body of Christ does not have a man as head.

III. The Body Is Subject to Its Head.

A. Ephesians 5:24
B. Just as the body is governed by every dictate of the head, we can only operate by the direction of Christ.

IV. The Body Is Made Up of Many Members.

A. 1 Corinthians 12:12-14
B. Romans 12:4-5
C. Ephesians 5:30
D. This will help us see that the work of an individual and the work of the church differ (1 Tim. 5:16).

V. The Body Is to Be Free from Division.

A. 1 Corinthians 12:25

B. Division is condemned in the Bible.
    1. 1 Corinthians 1:10
    2. 1 Corinthians 11:17-18
C. Unity was the prayer of Jesus (John 17:20-21).
D. We must endeavor to keep unity in the body of Christ (Eph. 4:3).

VI. The Body Is the Place of Reconciliation.

A. Ephesians 2:16
B. Colossians 1:20-22
C. Sin separates man from God (Isa. 59:1-2).

VII. The Body Is Entered By Baptism.

A. 1 Corinthians 12:13
B. The only means an individual has of entering the one body is by baptism.
C. Baptism is a burial in water for the remission of past sins (Acts 2:38; 8:36-38).

Conclusion

1. Christ is the savior of the body (Eph. 5:23).
2. Are you a member of the one body?

Five Houses

Introduction

1. The Bible speaks of a number of houses. The word "house" is used in different ways in God's Word.
2. Let's look at "Five Houses."

Discussion

I. Our Homes – The Family.

A. Luke 16:27 – ". . . my father's house"
B. 1 Timothy 3:12 – ". . . ruling . . . their own houses well"
C. Hebrews 11:7 – ". . . to the saving of his house. . . ."
D. Genesis 18:19 – ". . . he will command . . . his household. . . ."
E. Acts 11:14; 10:2; 16:31 – speaks of Cornelius and the prison keeper's house.

II. A Dwelling Place.

A. The place we reside is called a house.
B. Luke 19:5
C. Matthew 9:6
D. Philemon 2 (explain ". . . church in thy house").
E. 1 Corinthians 11:22, 34; Romans 14:17

III. Our Physical Bodies – An Earthly House.

A. 2 Corinthians 5:1-6
B. 2 Corinthians 4:16-18
C. James 2:26
D. Our physical bodies are but a house for that which is eternal, our soul.

IV. A Spiritual House.

A. 1 Peter 2:5
B. Read and study 1 Peter 2:5-10.
C. 1 Timothy 3:15 teaches us that God's house is the church.
D. 1 Corinthians 3:16; Ephesians 2:22; Hebrews 3:6; Psalm 23:6; Isaiah 2:2-3

E. The Lord's house is made up of living stones, individual Christians, forming a spiritual house.

V. This House.

A. This building is a meeting-house for the Lord's people in this community.

B. This building is not the church (Acts 5:11; 1 Cor. 14:23).

C. Even though this house is not a spiritual house and we know that God does not dwell in temples made by hands (Acts 17:24), there must be some respect for this building which was paid for with money given to do the Lord's work.

D. It is in this house that we:

1. Sing (Heb. 2:12; Eph. 5:19).
2. Pray (Acts 12:5; 2:42).
3. Give (1 Cor. 16:2).
4. Eat the Lord's Supper (1 Cor. 11:23-34).
5. Teach the Word of God (1 Thess. 1:8).
6. Hear the name of Christ confessed and see folks being baptized into Christ (Rom. 6:3-4; Gal. 3:27).

Conclusion

Won't you come to be a part of the Lord's house?

Where Planning Is Needed

Introduction

1. Where there is little planning, little gets done.
2. Millions spent by business on research and development for future products.
3. Some areas where planning is needed:

Discussion

I. In Our Giving.

A. 1 Corinthians 16:1-2

B. 2 Corinthians 9:7

C. To give liberally we must make the proper plans.

D. Need to give "off the top" and not our leftovers.

II. In Marriage.

A. Not just in the typical wedding arrangements.

B. Marriage involves a life-long commitment (Rom. 7:2).

C Some spend more time in buying a car or house than in selecting a life-long companion.

D. Divorce rate is alarming.

E. How to plan for marriage:

1. By being mature and ready for marriage.
2. By marrying someone who has a right to marry (Matt. 19:9).
3. By choosing someone who is compatible.

F. Parents need to teach their children about responsibilities in marriage.

G. Important to marry a faithful Christian.

III. In Appointing Church Leaders.

A. Planning for church leaders will help to solve the problems of churches going for years without elders.

B. Planning must be done to appoint only qualified men (1 Tim. 3; Tit. 1).

C. Young and middle age men must plan to be elders and deacons in the Lord's church. There is a great need.

D. Paul planned for elders (Acts 14:23).
E. ". . . If a man desire the office of a bishop, he desireth a good work" (1 Tim. 3:1) and deacons ". . .well purchase to themselves a good degree. . ." (1 Tim. 3:13).

IV. In the Work of the Church.

A. If the church is to do its work successfully it must be planned.
B. Notice the Lord's plan for the teaching of the gospel in Acts 1:8 (Jerusalem, Judaea, Samaria, and uttermost part of the earth).
C. There were plans made when some widows were found neglected (Acts 6:1-6).
D. The plans we make for the future show our faith in it.
E. Ralph Waldo Emerson said, "Where there is no vision a people perish."
F. Planning needed in all areas of the work: evangelism, restoring the erring, discipline, gospel meetings, Bible classes, etc.
G. Both short-term and long-range plans are important.

V. In Our Lives.

A. Many live from day to day and have no concern for the future.
B. Ephesians 5:15-16
C. Many too busy "making a living" to live.
D. Take time for the important things: God, worship, Bible study, working for the Lord, being with your family, etc.
E. Psalm 90:12

Conclusion

Are you planning for eternity?

Pleasant Things

Introduction

1. Text: Isaiah 64:11
2. This text helps us to appreciate that there were, and are, some pleasant things; things that are esteemed and/or are pleasing.
3. Let's notice a few *pleasant things* in our study.

Discussion

I. The Unity of Brethren.

- A. Psalm 133:1
- B. Unity is that for which we must constantly strive.
- C. 1 Corinthians 1:10
- D. Must endeavor to keep (Eph. 4:3).
- E. Philippians 1:27; 2:2
- F. Unity can be enjoyed when we all walk by the same rule (Phil. 3:16).

II. Wisdom and Knowledge.

- A. Proverbs 3:17
- B. Knowledge is pleasant to the soul (Prov. 2:10).
- C. Wisdom and knowledge that come from God are the greatest kind and that for which we should long! (1 Cor. 3:18).
- D. Proverbs 19:8, 20
- E. James asked, "Who is a wise man?" (Jas. 3:13).
- F. Paul prayed for such in the case of the Colossians (Col. 1:9-10).

III. Some People.

- A. Some, in God's Word, were said to be pleasant.
- B. In David's lament, he said, "Saul and Jonathan were lovely and pleasant in their lives. . ." (2 Sam. 1:23).
- C. David, speaking of Jonathan, said, ". . . very pleasant hast thou been unto me: thy love to me was wonderful. . ." (2 Sam. 1:26).
- D. It's nice to be around pleasant people and to have pleasant friends. God's

people should be pleasant to be around and make for pleasant friends!

IV. Singing Praises.

A. Psalm 135:3; 147:1

B. Ephesians 5:19

C. Singing is something that we should enjoy and appreciate as a pleasant thing.

D. The apostle said, "I will sing with the spirit and I will sing with the understanding also" (1 Cor. 14:15).

V. The Words of the Pure.

A. Proverbs 15:26

B. Proverbs 16:24

C. These words that we speak are both pleasant to God and should be pleasant to others also.

D. Our words are important! (Eccl. 3:7; Phil. 1:27; Col. 4:6; Matt. 12:37).

VI. A Child.

A. God asked, "Is Ephraim my dear son? Is he a pleasant child?" (Jer. 31:20).

B. God, at this time, was concerned about the tribe of Ephraim and spoke of Ephraim as His "dear son" and asked is he (Ephraim) "a pleasant child?"

C. A pleasant child is one who is obedient to God and seeks to do His will at all times. Are you, as a child of God, a pleasant child (Gal. 3:26)?

D. Are you as a child, in the family relationship, a pleasant child (Eph. 6:1-2)?

VII. Our Offerings.

A. Malachi 3:4

B. This newly refined priesthood that Malachi spoke of (Mal. 3:3) is the spiritual priesthood under the New Covenant (1 Pet. 2:5, 9), whose sacrifices are those of praise and thanksgiving. They are the fruit of lips that makes confession to His name, a confession and praise that flow from a pure heart (Heb. 13:15-16).

C. Our offerings, the offerings of the redeemed, are pleasant and acceptable to God (Rom. 12:1).

D. We should, as Christ did, offer ourselves to God for a sweet smelling savour (Eph. 5:2).

Conclusion

1. Why don't you come today and offer yourself in obedience to the One who loves you and sought your salvation.
2. Your decision to obey the Lord will most certainly be a pleasant one! Come now!

I Can

Introduction

1. Philippians 4:13
2. We need to put into our minds the concept of I can.

Discussion

I. I Can Overcome Temptation.

A. Some think they just can't overcome temptation.

B. We can overcome temptation (1 Cor. 10:13).

1. Temptation is common in that all men are tempted the same way (1 John 2:16).
2. We will not be given temptation that we cannot overcome.
3. The Lord provides a way of escape.

C. A blessing for those who overcome (Jas. 1:12-15).

II. I Can Change.

A. Some think they are too old and set in their ways – that they can't make a change.

B. Repentance means to change.

1. Matthew 21:28-30
2. Acts 17:30
3. 2 Peter 3:9

C. Examples of some who did change.

1. Murderers (Acts 2).
2. Sorcerers (Acts 8:9-13).
3. Blasphemers (1 Tim. 1:13).
4. The grossly immoral (1 Cor. 6:9-11).

D. The gospel has power to change (Rom. 1:16).

III. I Can Teach Others.

A. Some think they don't know enough to teach others.

B. You never come to a point where you know it all!

C. Andrew first brought his brother to Jesus (John 1:40-42).
D. Paul straightway preached Christ (Acts 9:20).
E. We are taught to teach (Matt. 28:19-20; 2 Tim. 2:2).

IV. I Can Make a Difference.

A. Some think they are alone and what they say doesn't matter – that they can't make a difference.
B. The Bible teaches the power of influence.
   1. Matthew 5:13-16
   2. 1 Corinthians 5:6
   3. 2 Corinthians 3:2
C. You can make a difference at school, at work, at home, and in the church!

V. I Can Be a Christian.

A. Some are not Christians because they think they can't be.
B. Christ died for every man (Heb. 2:9; 1 John 2:2),
C. You're invited to be a Christian (Matt. 11:28-30).
D. You can be a Christian!

VI. I Can Understand the Bible.

A. Some have been made to believe that they just can't understand the Bible.
B. We are commanded to understand (Eph. 5:17).
C. Paul taught that when we read the Bible we can understand it (Eph. 3:4).
D. Need to study so we may understand (2 Tim. 2:15).

VII. I Can Go to Heaven.

A. Some think that God requires too much and that there is just no way they can make it to Heaven.
B. Christ never said it would be easy (Matt. 7:13-14).
C. If you have the desire to go to Heaven, you can go!
D. We must be faithful to the Lord (Rev. 2:10).

Conclusion

1. I can, if I think I can!
2. You can become a Christian now as we stand and sing.

Right Things About the Church

Introduction

1. Much confusion concerning New Testament church.
2. Let's look at some right things about the church of Christ.

Discussion

I. Started at the Right Place.

A. Jerusalem

B. Isaiah 2:2-3; Jeremiah 3:14-18; Zechariah 1:16

C. Acts 2:5

II. Started at the Right Time.

A. Isaiah 2:2-3 – ". . . in the last days. . . ."

B. Acts 2:16-17 – "But this is that. . ." (Joel 2:28-32).

C. Hebrews 1:1-3

III. We Have the Right People.

A. Jews (Acts 2:5).

B. Romans 1:16

IV. The Right Power.

A. Holy Spirit.

B. Mark 9:1 – a promise to the apostles (John 16:13).

C. Acts 1:4-8; 2:1-4

D. Luke 24:49

E. Gospel power to save (Rom. 1:16).

V. The Right Preachers.

A. The apostles (2 Cor. 4:7).

B. Matthew 16:19; 18:18

C. 2 Corinthians 5:18-20

VI. The Right Headship.

A. Christ.

B. Colossians 1:18
C. Ephesians 1:22-23
D. Denominations have human heads.

VII. The Right Standard of Authority.

A. Matthew 28:18-20
B. The Bible is God's complete and final revelation to man (2 Tim. 3:16-17; Jude 3).

VIII. The Right Work.

A. 1 Thessalonians 1:8
B. The work of the church is given to us by Christ and is of a spiritual nature. It involves:
   1. Preaching the gospel (1 Thess. 1:8; Matt. 28:19-20).
   2. Helping needy saints (Rom. 15:25-26; 1 Tim. 5:16).
   3. Teaching Christians (Acts 20:32; Eph. 4:11-16).
C. 1 Corinthians 11:22

IX. The Right Worship.

A. Acts 2:42
B. The church worships in spirit and in truth (John 4:24).
C. Matthew 15:9

X. The Right Destiny.

A. 1 Corinthians 15:23-24
B. At the end of time the church will be delivered up to God!
C. We sing, "this world is not my home. . . ."

Conclusion

Why not become a member of the right church today?

Faithfulness

Introduction

1. Text: Revelation 2:10
2. Baptism is not the end, but the beginning (1 Cor. 15:58).
3. Let's notice some areas in which we need faithfulness.

Discussion

I. Worshipping God.

A. Matthew 4:10

B. 1 Peter 2:5

C. Not to forsake assembling as the Lord's people have come together to worship (Heb. 10:25).

D. Acts 2:42

E. Ways we worship:

1. Lord's supper (Acts 20:7).
2. Giving (1 Cor. 16:2).
3. Preaching (2 Tim. 4:2).
4. Prayer (1 Thess. 5:17).
5. Singing (Eph. 5:19).

F. Must worship in spirit and in truth (John 4:24).

II. Moral Purity.

A. Live in a world of immorality, with sensuality, pornography, indecent dress, filthy talk, etc.

B. 1 John 2:15-17; Titus 2:12

C. Galatians 5:22

D. James 1:27

E. Christians are to live pure lives (1 Tim. 5:22).

F. "Abstain from all appearance of evil" (1 Thess. 5:22).

G. We need to teach our children correct moral values (Eph. 6:4).

III. Bearing Fruit.

A. John 15:1-8
B. Fruit trees of no value unless they bear fruit.
C. Christians are to bear fruit, "much fruit" (John 15:8) and such is a test of true discipleship.
D. Those who don't bear fruit will be taken away!
E. Bear fruit by:
   1. Being zealous of good works (Tit. 2:14; Matt. 5:16; Col. 1:10).
   2. Being involved in the Lord's work (1 Cor. 15:58; Eph. 4:16).
   3. Leading others to Christ (2 Tim. 2:2; Gal. 6:1).
F. We can bear fruit by putting our abilities to use in the Lord's kingdom (Matt. 25).
G. We can't stand up for Jesus if we're sitting down in the Lord's vineyard!

Conclusion

1. It's easy for folks to depart and not be faithful.
2. 2 Peter 2:20-22

Selling Your Birthright for a Mess of Pottage

Introduction

1. Genesis 25-27 records the story of Esau (the son of Isaac and elder to Jacob). Famished, he exchanged his rights as firstborn for a "mess of pottage" or red lentil stew. Esau exchanged that which was considered of great value (his birthright that gave privileges of high value) for something of considerably less value, a "mess of pottage."
2. I'm wondering if perhaps we don't, at times, do the very same as Esau; that is, exchange something of great and lasting value for a moment of pleasure.
3. Let's notice some ways that we can *exchange* our birthright for a "mess of pottage."

Discussion

I. Exchange Bible Study.

- A. Bible study has great and lasting value.
  1. Promotes spiritual growth (2 Pet. 3:18; 1:3).
  2. Profitable (2 Tim. 3:16-17). We have within the Bible "all things that pertain unto life and godliness. . ." (1 Pet. 1:3).
  3. Equips us to recognize false doctrine (1 John 4:1).
  4. Prepares one for the judgment (John 12:48; Rom. 2:16).
  5. Helps to make us approved of God (2 Tim. 2:15).
- B. The noble Bereans searched the scriptures *daily* (Acts 17:11).
- C. Folks today exchange many things for Bible study. They exchange Bible study for secular reading, watching TV, listening to popular music, sleeping, recreation or entertainment, etc. Few spend very much time studying and learning from God's Word.
- D. To exchange Bible study for these things is like selling your birthright for a "mess of pottage."

II. Exchange Worship.

A. Few people today put emphasis on worship!
B. God is to be worshipped (Ps. 29:2; 100:1-5; Luke 4:8).
C. We are to worship in spirit and in truth (John 4:24).
D. The apostle of the Lord instructed Christians, "not forsaking the assembling of ourselves together . . . but exhorting one another" (Heb. 10:25).
E. To exchange worship for whatever is like selling your birthright for a mess of pottage! The worship of God is important and has lasting benefits!

III. Exchange the Spiritual Nurturing of Your Children.

A. Parents have responsibility (Eph. 6:4).
B. Children need spiritual training as well as physical training! This is most often neglected.
C. Most parents, who are members of the church, don't even think much about it until their children go astray. Then it may be too late!
D. Israel was told about its importance (Deut. 11:19).
E. Children need to be trained in the way they should go (Prov. 22:6).
F. To exchange the spiritual nurturing of your children is like selling your birthright for a mess of pottage. You may, as Esau of old, weep bitterly when you realize how important this spiritual training is!

IV. Exchange Your Good Name.

A. A good name is valuable (Prov. 22:1; Eccl. 7:1).
B. Sometimes a parent will warn a child about ruining his good name through wrongdoings.
C. Once a good name is blemished, it's virtually impossible to reestablish it!
D. Some folks will spend nearly a life-time building a good name and then exchange it for a moment of temporal pleasure. We've all known of members who were guilty of the sin of adultery and exchanged their good name.
E. Don't exchange your good name for anything! It would be a poor bargain, like selling your birthright for a mess of pottage!

V. Exchange the Opportunity to Give to the Lord.

A. To be able to give to the Lord is one of the great blessings of a child of God.
B. Acts 20:35
C. 2 Corinthians 9:6
D. 1 Corinthians 16:1-2
E. Some exchange the opportunity and privilege to give to the Lord and further the cause of the Lord Jesus Christ by spending their money foolishly. Compare the money you spend on physical things in contrast to that which you give to the Lord. Most people "waste" more money than they ever give to the Lord!
F. Giving to the Lord says something about what comes first in your life.

G. The poor widow's example (Mark 12:41-44).
H. Don't exchange giving to the Lord. It would be like Esau of old who sold his birthright for a mess of pottage.

VI. Exchange Your Talents That Can Be Used in the Lord's Service.

A. We all have various talents that can be used in the Lord's service. No one is talentless!
B. Some have talents, but are afraid to use them like the one talent man (Matt. 25:25).
C. What better way to serve the Lord than to apply yourself to gaining certain talents that will be useful in serving Him. We apply ourselves to developing abilities in physical areas.
D. Rather than learning and using talents that will be of benefit to the Lord, many exchange it for some ability that will only be of help to them physically.
E. To exchange your talents that can be used in the Lord's service is like selling your birthright for a mess of pottage.

VII. Exchange the Kingdom of God.

A. The kingdom or church is to come first (Matt. 6:33).
B. We, as the kingdom of the Lord, are His bride and we must put Him first as a bride would her husband. The bridegroom (Christ) will accept nothing less.
C. Far too many consider the church of our Lord unimportant. Few even consider church membership important today.
D. The kingdom of God is that which will be, at the end, delivered up to God (1 Cor. 15:24).
E. The kingdom is compared to a pearl of great value (Matt. 13:45-46).
F. Don't exchange the kingdom or church for anything! To exchange it for anything is like selling your birthright for a mess of pottage.

Conclusion

1. The Bible says that Esau "despised his birthright." That is, he did not appreciate its value or looked lightly upon it. Don't despise these things of great importance by exchanging them for things of little significance eternally.
2. Esau not only despised his birthright, but lost his blessing as well and "cried with a great and exceeding bitter cry. . ." (Gen. 27:34).
3. Far too many realize too late that they are selling their birthright for a mess of pottage.

Bible Parents With Troubling Children

Introduction

1. A lot of parents today are having trouble with their children.
2. This is not a new problem. Many parents of the Bible experienced trouble with their children. Thus, we study.

Discussion

I. Adam and Eve Had Trouble with Cain.

A. Adam and Eve were the parents of three sons: Cain, Abel, and Seth (Gen. 4:1-2, 25).

B. Cain murdered his brother, Abel (Gen. 4:8).

C. Adam and Eve brought sin into the world before their children (Gen. 2:16-17; 3:1-24).

II. Noah Had Trouble with Ham.

A. Noah was the father of three sons: Shem, Ham, and Japheth (Gen. 5:32).

B. Ham saw his father's nakedness and told his two brothers with delight (Gen. 9:20-27).

C. Noah was drunk with wine and lay naked in his tent and thus provided temptation to Ham.

III. Lot Had Trouble with Daughters.

A. Lot's daughters made him drink wine and committed sexual immorality with him (Gen. 19:30-38).

B. Lot dwelled near Sodom, an exceedingly wicked city (Gen. 13:5-14).

C. Parents need to realize the influence of evil companions on their children (1 Cor. 15:33).

IV. Isaac and Rebekah Had Trouble with Jacob.

A. Jacob and Esau were the twin sons born to Isaac and Rebekah (Gen. 25:19-

26).

B. Jacob took the birthright from Esau (Gen. 25:27-34).
C. Jacob obtained the blessing by deception (Gen. 27).
D. Isaac and Rebekah showed favoritism.

V. Jacob Had Trouble with Sons.

A. Jacob's sons sold Joseph (Gen. 37:13-28).
B. Jacob was partial to Joseph (Gen. 37:3-4).
C. Parents might avoid some trouble with their children by showing the same love for all their children.

VI. Eli Had Trouble with Sons.

A. Eli's sons lay with the women that assembled at the door of the tabernacle (1 Sam. 2:12, 22).
B. Eli did not restrain his sons (1 Sam. 3:13).
C. Parents need to see the importance of disciplining their children (Prov. 22:6, 15; Eph. 6:4).

VII. An Israelitish Woman Had Trouble with Son.

A. Son blasphemed the Lord's name (Lev. 24:10-16).
B. The law forbade profaning God's name (Exod. 20:7).
C. Parents must teach their children respect for God.

VIII. The Israelites Had Trouble with Children.

A. Their children did not know the Lord and served false gods (Judg. 2:10-13).
B. Israel did not teach their children, nor did they guard against evil influences.

IX. Aaron Had Trouble with Sons.

A. Leviticus 10:1-2
B. The sons of Aaron perverted God's worship and were struck dead by God.
C. Parents need to teach their children the importance of worshipping as God directs.

Conclusion

1. Much of the trouble Bible parents had with their children was brought on by themselves.
2. It is important that parents and children have the proper relationship.

"The People Who Know Their God"

Introduction

1. Text: Daniel 11:32
2. Men are admonished to know God (1 Chron. 28:9; Jer. 9:23-24; John 6:45; Heb. 8:11; John 17:3).
3. There are consequences for not knowing God (Rom. 1:28-29).
4. Let's notice characteristics of those who know God.

Discussion

I. Are Strong and Take a Stand.

A. Daniel 11:32 – "exploits" (takes action).

B. God has always required His people to be strong (Josh. 1:6-9; 2 Pet. 1:5).

C. Ephesians 6:10-14

1. Stand for truth and right.
2. Stand against the wiles of the devil.

D. 1 John 4:17

II. Pray.

A. Daniel 6:4-5 – tried to find fault against Daniel.

B. Decree made concerning prayer (Dan. 6:7).

C. Notice Daniel 6:10-11. Daniel could have reasoned that it would not hurt to just miss one month.

D. Daniel 9:3-4

E. 1 Thessalonians 5:17; Ephesians 6:18; Philippians 4:6-7; 1 Timothy 2:8

III. Have Faith in God.

A. Daniel 6:23

B. Daniel 6:26 – Even caused King Darius to have respect for God.

C. Daniel 4:17 – God rules in the kingdoms of men.

D. Hebrews 11:6; Acts 27:25; 2 Timothy 1:12

IV. Obey God Regardless of the Consequences.

A. Relate circumstances of Daniel 3.
B. King Nebuchadnezzar's golden image (Dan. 3:10-11).
C. Shadrach, Meshach, and Abednego (Dan. 3:16-18; 19-30).
D. Philemon 8; Hebrews 1:14; Ephesians 6:20
E. Daniel 3:17-18 – content with God's way!

V. Will Not Compromise.

A. Daniel 3:17-18
B. Moses (Exod. 10:26; Josh. 24:15).
C. Galatians 2:4-5; Job 13:15

VI. Find the Time to Worship God.

A. Daniel 6:10
B. Daniel 3:5-6, 17, 28
C. Matthew 4:8-10; John 4:24; Revelation 22:8-9; Matthew 15:9; Acts 2:42; Ephesians 5:19

VII. Are Bold.

A. Boldness is the spirit of those who know their God!
B. The boldness of Shadrach, Meshach, and Abednego (Dan. 3:6, 18).
C. Daniel in the lions' den (Dan. 6).
D. Paul (Acts 20:22-27; 4:29; Phil. 1:14-20; 1 Thess. 2:2; Phile. 8; 1 John 4:17; Eph. 6:20).

VIII. Purpose in Their Hearts.

A. Daniel 1:8
B. We need to make up our minds before temptation comes our way!
C. 1 Corinthians 10:13; Acts 11:23
D. 2 Corinthians 9:6-7

Conclusion

Why not come and take your stand today?

Lessons Learned From a Desert Encounter

Introduction

1. Two men met, but not by chance, on a desert road.
2. This meeting resulted in a child of God being born.
3. Philip and the eunuch (Acts 8:26-39).
4. What lessons can be learned from this desert encounter?

Discussion

I. The Work of the Holy Spirit.

- A. Many confused about His work.
- B. The Spirit told the preacher to go join himself to the eunuch's chariot (Acts 8:28).
- C. No direct operation of the Holy Spirit on the sinner!
- D. When Philip got to the eunuch as a result of the Spirit's bidding, he "began at the same scripture" (Acts 8:35).
- E. The Spirit works through the Word of God today (Eph. 5:17; 1 Tim. 4:1; Eph. 3:5; 1 Cor. 2:14).

II. The Work of Preachers.

- A. Philip, the preacher, ". . .began at the same scripture, and preached unto him Jesus" (Acts 8:35).
- B. The work of preachers involves preaching the Word (2 Tim. 4:2).
- C. Preachers are limited as to what they can preach – the Word!
- D. Notice that Philip preached, in this case, to only one man. Don't have to have great multitudes!
- E. He started where the eunuch was (Acts 8:32-35) and he knew this by having been a good listener (Acts 8:30).

III. That Baptism Is a Part of Preaching Jesus.

- A. When Philip preached Jesus (Acts 8:35) the eunuch asked, "What doth hinder me to be baptized?" (Acts 8:36).

B. The eunuch asked about baptism for such is involved in preaching Christ (Acts 8:12).
C. Most leave out baptism.
D. Peter's sermon on Pentecost included baptism for the remission of sins (Acts 2:38).

IV. The Necessity of Faith.

A. The necessity of faith is seen in the fact that Philip answered the eunuch's question, ". . . what doth hinder me to be baptized?" (Acts 8:36) with ". . . If thou believest with all thine heart, thou mayest" (Acts 8:37).
B. Before the eunuch was baptized he confessed his faith, ". . . I believe that Jesus Christ is the Son of God" (Acts 8:37).
C. Faith is essential to being saved (Heb. 11:6; John 8:24; Mark 16:16).

V. What One Confesses.

A. Most confess their sins or what God has done for them.
B. The eunuch confessed, ". . . I believe that Jesus Christ is the Son of God" (Acts 8:37).
C. Romans 10:10; Matthew 10:32
D. Notice that this is a public confession.

VI. What Baptism Is.

A. Baptism involves, in Acts 8, a coming to the water (Acts 8:36), a going into the water (Acts 8:38), and a coming up out of the water (Acts 8:39).
B. This is the baptism of the great commission (Mark 16:15-16) and the baptism of Ephesians 4:4.
C. No need to argue about this being a desert place for the Scriptures say that he was baptized or immersed (Matt. 14:13)!
D. Other things were involved in his baptism:
   1. Understanding (Acts 8:30).
   2. Urgency (Acts 8:36-39).

VII. The Joy of Being a Christian.

A. Upon the eunuch becoming a Christian he "went on his way rejoicing" (Acts 8:39).
B. He had received the promise of the Lord (Mark 16:16).
C. He had his past sins forgiven (Acts 2:38; Rom. 3:25).
D. Matthew 5:12
E. ". . . Rejoice in the Lord. . ." (Phil. 3:1).

Conclusion

1. Your "encounter" doesn't have to be a desert one!
2. Come today.

Shewing Forth the Praises of God

Introduction

1. Text: 1 Peter 2:9
2. Peter is speaking of God's chosen people, and says that we have been redeemed so that we might shew forth (or proclaim, ASV) the praise (or excellencies, ASV) of God. Since this is God's purpose in calling us, how is it that Christians proclaim the praises of God?

Discussion

I. By Becoming A Christian, We Shew Forth His Praises.

A. This is where it all begins! Peter says, "But ye are a chosen generation, a royal priesthood, an holy nation, a peculiar people; *that ye. . . .*"

B. The old man is crucified and the new man is a follower of Jesus Christ (Rom. 6:4-6; Eph. 4:22-32).

C. The name that we wear, "Christian," shows forth His praises. It is the "new name" by which God's people are called (Isa. 66:2; Acts 11:26).

D. One becomes a Christian by HBRCB.

E. One cannot show forth His praises or excellencies if he is not a Christian!

II. By Praising God in Worship, We Shew Forth His Praises.

A. John 4:24

B. Ephesians 3:21 – Unto Him be glory in the church.

C. For this reason we should not forsake the assembling (Heb. 10:25).

D. God is worthy of our praise, devotion, and worship.

III. By Teaching God's Excellent Ways to Others, We Shew Forth His Praises.

A. 2 Timothy 2:2

B. 1 Peter 3:15 – We need to be ready to give answer.

C. Hebrews 5:12 – We "ought to be teachers..."

D. Matthew 28:19-20 - The apostles were commissioned to go teach, baptize, and teach.
E. Acts 8:4 – The early persecuted disciples went every where preaching the Word.
F. We should instill His ways in our children (Eph. 6:4).

IV. By Living a Consistently Faithful Life, We Shew Forth His Praises.

A. 1 Corinthians 15:58
B. Colossians 1:23
C. Hypocrisy is a grievous sin (Matt. 23).
D. We must "walk in the light" (1 John 1:7).
E. Revelation 2:10
F. We should *ever* be showing forth His praises and excellencies!

V. By Being Filled with Good Works, We Shew Forth His Praises.

A. Matthew 5:16 – As men see our good works, they glorify the Father in Heaven.
B. Acts 9:36 – Dorcas was full of good works.
C. 1 Timothy 6:18 – We should be rich in good works.
D. Titus 2:14; 3:1, 8, 14
E. God's praises or excellencies are seen in us as we go about doing good works!

Conclusion

1. All that we do is to reveal and reflect the excellencies of our Father (and His Son), to mirror His righteousness and goodness.
2. With redemption comes the responsibility to "shew forth his praises."
3. May we not be like the sand of the sea that sucks up the rain and bears no flowers; but let us give back to God in praise what His love and mercy have given us.
4. What are you proclaiming?

The Great Commission

Introduction

1. The Lord has given commissions to different people in different ages of time.
2. The commission found in Matthew 28:18-20; Mark 16:15-16; Luke 24:46-47 is known as the great commission.
3. Let's notice the greatness of this commission.

Discussion

I. Great Authority of Jesus.

   A. Matthew 28:18
   B. Matthew 7:29
   C. John 2:5
   D. This great authority was given unto Jesus by His Father (1 Cor. 15:27; Eph. 1:21-23).

II. Great Charge.

   A. Matthew 28:19
   B. Mark 16:15
   C. There is no greater charge than the charge to go teach!
   D. This is the only way men have of knowing the will of God (John 6:44-45).
   E. We have been given this great charge (2 Tim. 2:2; 4:2).

III. Great Group of People.

   A. All nations are to be taught (Matt. 28:19; Luke 24:47).
   B. The gospel is for all the world (Mark 16:15).
   C. This commission is not limited to a certain ethnic group, but is for all people in every nation!

IV. Great Message.

   A. The great message is the gospel of Christ (Mark 16:15).
   B. The gospel is God's power to save men from their sins (Rom. 1:16; 1 Cor. 15:1-2).

C. In preaching the gospel, the apostles would preach repentance and remission of sins in the Lord's name (Luke 24:47).

V. Great Plan of Salvation.

A. Mark 16:16

B. God's plan is simple: Belief + Baptism = Salvation.

C. The Lord's plan for keeping the saved, saved is continual teaching (Matt. 28:19-20).

VI. Great Promise.

A. Matthew 28:20

B. The Lord has promised to be with us!

C. The Lord was with the apostle Paul (Acts 18:9-10).

D. No wonder early Christians were motivated to go everywhere preaching the Word (Acts 8:4).

VII. Great Beginning.

A. Luke 24:47

B. The great commission was executed for the first time on Pentecost when the apostles preached the gospel to all nations (Acts 2).

C. This brought about the greatest institution known to mankind – the Lord's church (Acts 2:47).

Conclusion

1. May we have a greater appreciation for the great commission.
2. Let us be zealous in carrying out the great commission given by our Lord.

Needed Preaching of the Twentieth Century

Introduction

1. Soft preaching seems to be the order of the day. Many speak softly and tread lightly.
2. New Testament preaching consisted of:

Discussion

I. Cut to the Heart Preaching.
   A. Acts 7:51-60 (v. 54).
   B. Study context.

II. Reproving, Rebuking, and Exhorting Preaching.
   A. 2 Timothy 4:1-5
   B. Discuss each point.

III. World Turning Preaching.
   A. Acts 17:1-6
   B. We need this today.

IV. Bold Preaching.
   A. Philippians 1:14
   B. Ephesians 6:19-20
   C. Acts 4:13
   D. Acts 9:27

V. Public and Private Preaching.
   A. Acts 20:17-20
   B. Takes both kinds!

VI. Heart Pricking Preaching.
   A. Acts 2:22-37

B. Only way to motivate people to do something is to get to the heart!

VII. In Season and Out of Season Preaching.

A. 2 Timothy 4:2
B. Never a time to let up!

VIII. Preaching Which Could Be Understood.

A. A lot of preaching today can't be understood by the average person in the pew.
B. Bible preaching must be understandable.
C. Nehemiah 8:4-8
D. Ephesians 5:17; 3:4
E. 2 Corinthians 11:3
F. Needs to be well organized so people can easily understand.

IX. Christ Centered Preaching.

A. Acts 8:5
B. Acts 8:35
C. 1 Corinthians 15:1-6

X. Soul Searching Preaching.

A. 2 Corinthians 13:5
B. Sermon that caused men to look into their own hearts.
C. We need to get enthused (Ezek. 6:11).

Conclusion

1. Some preaching does not have the profit that other preaching has (Heb. 4:2).
2. You can't improve on this kind of preaching!

The Parable of the Great Supper

Introduction

1. Text: Luke 14:15-24
2. Let's draw five lessons from this great supper parable.

Discussion

I. God Makes Ready Our Salvation and Invites Us to Come.

A. In parable, man made great supper and bade many (Luke 14:16).

B. To make a "great supper" takes a great deal of preparation (Gal. 4:4-5).

C. God has prepared salvation for mankind (1 Pet. 1:18-23; Eph. 3:10-11). This preparation involved grace, love, mercy, Jesus, Jesus' blood, the gospel, etc.

D. We are invited to this great feast, ". . . Come; for all things are now ready" (Luke 14:17).

E. As in such cases, we only have the right to be at the feast at the invitation of the host (Matt. 11:28-30; Rev. 22:17).

II. There Is Joy in God's Kingdom.

A. The idea of a great supper suggests joy and delight.

B. There is joy in the kingdom of God (Rom. 14:17).

C. Paul taught that we rejoice in the Lord (Phil. 3:1; 4:4).

D. Some view the kingdom like a long, dreary, funeral procession!

E. Revelation 22:14; Proverbs 16:20

F. We can even ". . . count it all joy when ye fall into divers temptations" (Jas. 1:2).

III. Jesus Wants Us Wholeheartedly.

A. Those bidden to the feast ". . . with one consent began to make excuse. . ." (Luke 14:18). Notice excuses.

B. ". . . None of those men which were bidden shall taste of my supper"

(Luke 14:24) – God demands our all!

C. Luke 14:26-27, 33; Matthew 10:37-38

D. Mark 12:30 – Heart, soul, mind, and strength involved.

E. Notice the end of those "... who mind earthly things" (Phil. 3:19).

IV. God Is Not Prejudiced.

A. Servant was told to bring in the poor, the maimed, the halt, the blind, and go into the highways and hedges and compel them to come in (Luke 14:21, 23).

B. Those originally bidden would have been the Jews and now the outcast and despised of the Jews, the pagan Gentiles, are invited to the feast.

C. "... Yet there is room" (Luke 14:22) – there is room in God's kingdom for all who will come!

D. There is no room for bigotry today. "There is neither Jew nor Greek, there is neither bond nor free, there is neither male nor female: for ye are all one in Christ Jesus" (Gal. 3:28).

E. Romans 2:12

F. Song: "The Gospel Is for All."

G. We must not prejudge who will and will not come to the feast (1 Cor. 1:26-29).

V. Rejection of God's Invitation Brings Exclusion.

A. ". . . None of those men which were bidden shall taste of my supper" (Luke 14:24).

B. Concerning those who chose not to go to the supper, it was said, "... none of those men which were bidden shall taste of my supper" (Luke 14:24).

C. To reject the Lord is to have the Lord reject us (Hosea 4:6) and to be "punished with everlasting destruction from the presence of the Lord, and from the glory of his power" (2 Thess. 1:9).

Conclusion

1. There is room for you in God's kingdom.
2. Won't you come to the feast?

“Purpose of Heart”

Introduction

1. Text: Daniel 1:8
2. Daniel is remembered as a youth who had purpose of heart. That is, he formed *a decided* purpose, and *meant* to carry it into effect as a matter of principle.
3. We need more Daniels’ today – folks who have purpose of heart, are determined to carry out the purpose as a matter of principle, and are determined not to defile themselves in any way.
4. Let’s notice some areas in which we need to have purpose of heart (resolve).

Discussion

I. Purpose to Abstain from Vices.

A. A vice is any immoral habit.
B. Your physical body is God-made (Gen. 2:7) and houses the immortal spirit (2 Cor. 5:1).
C. 1 Corinthians 6:20
D. The sin of fornication is one that you commit against your own body (1 Cor. 6:18-19) and no “fornicator . . . shall inherit the kingdom of God” (1 Cor. 6:10). See Hebrews 13:4.
E. Purpose in your heart to abstain from nicotine, all illicit drugs, alcohol, and any immoral habit. Determine to be a slave to none, except Jesus Christ.
F. Don’t be a partaker of others’ sins (1 Tim. 5:22).

II. Purpose to Keep Your Speech Pure.

A. Don’t use the mouth that God made to profane His name. His name is to be Hallowed (Matt. 6:9).
B. Purpose with your mouth (Ps. 17:3).
C. Blessing and cursing out of the same mouth? (Jas. 3:10).
D. Your speech should be always with grace (Col. 4:6).
E. Use sound speech (Tit. 2:6-8).

F. Don't speak evil of any man (Tit. 3:2).
G. Use your speech to herald out the praise of God (1 Pet. 2:9).

III. Purpose to Cleave unto the Lord.

A. Acts 11:23
B. "Cleave" means to abide with. This assumes that one is a Christian.
C. Barnabas exhorted these Christians to abide with, or cling, to the Lord and never depart from following Him. Abide in His doctrine (2 John 9).
D. We all need the purpose of heart that Hezekiah had (2 Kings 18:6).
E. Be determined to never leave Him or forsake Him!

IV. Purpose to Marry a Faithful Christian.

A. Perhaps no decision, other than your decision to obey the gospel, is of more importance..
B. Find and marry someone who will help you do the Lord's will and won't hinder.
C. ". . . Heirs together of the grace of life. . ." (1 Pet. 3:7).
D. The search may be long and hard, but be patient and pray for God's help.

V. Purpose to Work in the Lord's Vineyard.

A. The Lord's church is in need of determined workers.
B. We sing, "To the Work."
C. There is much to be done in spreading the gospel of Christ and workers are urgently needed everywhere. Be always abounding in the work (1 Cor. 15:58).
D. The church is compared to a vineyard to suggest that it is a place of work (Matt. 21:28).
E. The fields are white unto harvest (John 4:35).
F. The church needs elders, deacons, preachers, and teachers (Eph. 4:11-12).

VI. Purpose to Go to Heaven When You Die.

A. No one will go to Heaven accidentally!
B. Heaven is a prepared place for a prepared people! Prepare yourself so as to go.
C. Abraham looked for a city whose builder and maker is God (Heb. 11:10).
D. Those who do His commandments have the right to enter (Rev. 22:14).
E. The city described (Rev. 21:23-27). Notice that nothing will enter into Heaven that defileth!

Conclusion

1. Base your purposes upon God's Word and then have the determination to carry them out.
2. ". . . I have purposed it, I will also do it" (Isa. 46:11).

Essentials for Spiritual Growth

Introduction

1. God expects His children to grow up and be strong.
    a. 1 Peter 2:2
    b. 2 Peter 3:18
2. Here are some things that are essential for spiritual growth.

Discussion

I. The New Birth.

A. John 3:1-7
B. The new birth is a prerequisite of spiritual growth.
C. We are begotten by the Spirit through the Word of God.
  1. 1 Peter 1:23
  2. 1 Corinthians 4:15
  3. James 1:18
D. Have you been born again?

II. Spiritual Food.

A. Many do not grow because of a lack of food.
B. The Word of God provides the spiritual nourishment that is essential for spiritual growth.
  1. 1 Peter 2:2
  2. Hebrews 5:12-14
C. We must hunger and thirst after righteousness (Matt. 5:6).

III. Regular Exercise.

A. Exercise is necessary for growth and development.
B. 1 Timothy 4:7
C. Hebrews 5:14
D. Have you been getting regular exercise?

IV. A Good Environment.

A. We must be in an environment that promotes spiritual growth.

B. 1 Corinthians 15:33
C. Proverbs 13:20
D. What kind of an environment are you in?

V. The Proper Weight.

A. Our weight is important (Dan. 5:27).
B. God will weigh each of us on the great scales.
  1. 1 Samuel 2:3
  2. Proverbs 16:2
C. How much do you weigh?

VI. Freedom From Disease.

A. Sin is a disease that keeps many from growing spiritually.
  1. Isaiah 59:1-2
  2. Romans 6:23
  3. James 1:14-15
B. We must remove sin from our lives.

VII. The Right Temperature.

A. Temperature is an indicator of health.
B. Revelation 3:14-16
C. We need to have a zeal that is on fire for the Lord (Tit. 2:14).
D. Have you checked your temperature lately?

VIII. Frequent Examinations.

A. 2 Corinthians 13:5
B. A good time to take an examination is during the Lord's supper (1 Cor. 11:28).
C. How long has it been since you had an exam?

Conclusion

1. How is your spiritual growth?
2. We urge you to begin growing by being born again as we stand and sing.

Glorious Things of the Bible

Introduction

1. The word "glorious" suggests that which is magnificent or valuable.
2. We want to notice six glorious things of the Bible.

Discussion

I. Glorious Gospel.

A. 1 Timothy 1:11

B. 2 Corinthians 4:1-6

C. 2 Corinthians 3:6-11

D. Why is the gospel said to be glorious?

1. God's power to save (Rom. 1:16).
2. Means of calling (2 Thess. 2:14).
3. Begets (1 Cor. 4:15).
4. God's promises are made known by the gospel (Eph. 3:6).
5. The truth which makes known our hope is in the gospel (Col. 1:5).

II. Glorious Church.

A. Ephesians 5:25-27

B. Why is the church said to be glorious?

1. God is glorified (Eph. 3:21).
2. Home of the saved (Acts 2:47; Eph. 5:23).
3. Glorious builder and head (Matt. 16:18; Eph. 5:27).
4. Glorious end (1 Cor. 15:23).

C. The church is the bride of Christ (Rev. 22:17).

III. Glorious Liberty.

A. Romans 8:21

B. Galatians 5:1, 13

C. Discuss the danger in taking too much liberty (2 John 9; Prov. 14:12; Isa. 55:8-9; 1 Pet. 2:16).

IV. Glorious Power of God.

A. Colossians 1:9-12; Matthew 22:29
B. 1 Corinthians 2:5
C. Some evidence of such:
    1. Hebrews 11:3
    2. 1 Corinthians 1:18
    3. Hebrews 4:12

V. Glorious Second Appearing of Christ.

A. Titus 2:11-15; 2 Timothy 4:6-8
B. Hebrews 9:28
C. Why will His coming be glorious?
    1. Will come in glory (Matt. 25:31).
    2. Salvation is connected with His coming (Heb. 9:28).
    3. It is His last coming (Acts 1:11).
    4. There will be rewards in connection with His coming (Matt. 16:27).

VI. Glorious Body Like Christ's.

A. Philippians 3:20-21
B. 1 John 3:1-3
C. 1 Corinthians 15:35-58; John 12:24

VII. Glorious Name of God.

A. Psalm 72:19
B. Isaiah 63:14

Conclusion

You're invited to accept the glorious gospel of Christ and become a member of His glorious church.

One of These Days

Introduction

1. Many intend to do some things "one of these days."
2. Procrastination is but the thief of time!
3. "One of these days I intend to. . . ."

Discussion

I. Give Up Smoking.

A. Smoking is a nasty, foul habit!
B. Nothing good about smoking.
C. Harmful to the body as it causes lung cancer and heart disease.
D. 1 Corinthians 6:19-20
E. Ruins a person's good influence.
F. When you're young you're "big" if you smoke and when you're old you're "big" if you can quit!

II. Give Up Drinking.

A. Proverbs 20:1
B. Proverbs 23:29-32
C. Drinking has ruined many lives and is a major health problem today.
D. Don't often hear about the horror stories that go with drinking.
E. Galatians 5:19-20
F. Abe Lincoln said, "alcohol has many defenders, but no defense!"

III. Go to Church.

A. The importance of the church is seen in the fact that Jesus died for the church (Acts 20:28).
B. The apostle exhorted Christians to not forsake the assembling together to worship (Heb. 10:25).
C. Many are too busy with other things.
D. We need to get our priorities straight (Matt. 6:33).
E. The story is told of a man who said he would go to church when he got all

straightened out. Finally, he got all straightened out (a corpse) and they had his funeral at the church building!

IV. Be More Faithful.

A. Some not nearly as faithful as they could be.
B. Many know that they ought to do better (Jas. 4:17).
C. John 15:4, 6, 8
D. 2 Peter 2:20-22
E. We need to make up our minds to live better and be more faithful.
F. Some have just enough religion to make themselves miserable!

V. Be More Active in the Lord's Work.

A. God expects His people to work.
B. Song: "I Want to Be a Worker for the Lord."
C. John 15:2
D. We sing, "There is much to do. . . ."
E. We all need to get involved and stay involved in the Lord's work (1 Cor. 15:58).
F. The Lord's work is of critical importance!

VI. Be Baptized.

A. We need to recognize that baptism is a part of God's plan of salvation (Mark 16:16).
B. Baptism puts one into Christ (Gal. 3:27), where salvation is (2 Tim. 2:10).
C. The first gospel sermon commanded baptism (Acts 2:38) and those who gladly received the Word were baptized (Acts 2:41).
D. Peter taught that baptism saves (1 Pet. 3:21).
E. ". . . Arise, and be baptized. . ." (Acts 22:16).

VII. Be Restored.

A. Some have obeyed, but have fallen away.
B. It's possible to fall away and be lost eternally (Gal. 5:4; 2 Pet. 2:20-22).
C. 1 John 1:9
D. Simon was told to ". . . repent . . . and pray . . . that the thought of thine heart may be forgiven thee" (Acts 8:22).
E. James taught, "Confess your faults one to another, and pray one for another, that ye may be healed. The effectual fervent prayer of a righteous man availeth much" (Jas. 5:16).

Conclusion

1. It's been said that "the road to hell is paved with good intentions!"
2. We must carry our intentions into actions (2 Thess. 1:8).
3. Our lives are but a vapour (Jas. 4:13-15) and "How shall we escape, if we neglect so great salvation. . . ?" (Heb. 2:3).

The Race Set Before Us

Introduction

1. While many today are familiar with the "greatest spectacle in racing," some are not nearly as informed about the greatest race of all, the race set before us for a crown of eternal life.
2. Text: Hebrews 12:1-2
3. Let's notice some things the Bible says about this race.

Discussion

I. We Must Run the Race.

A. We need to be running this race for it is the greatest race of all, the race for eternal life (Heb. 12:1).

B. Before you can run the race, you must enter the race. We all enter the race the same way (HBRCB).

C. This race has been "set before us," that is, literally, "marked out for us." This race is marked out in God's Word. It tells us about the need for the race, how to enter the race, and then how to run.

II. We Are Compassed About with a Great Cloud of Witnesses.

A. We must run the race "seeing we . . . are compassed about with so great a cloud of witnesses" (Heb. 12:1).

B. In Hebrews 11, we have the example of many noble and faithful, who, under the severest trials, had run the race with patient endurance.

C. The apostle uses the example of those noble witnesses to encourage us to "run with patience the race that is set before us" (Heb. 12:1).

D. This "cloud of witnesses" ran a good race and obtained a good report through faith (Heb. 11:39).

III. We Must Lay Aside Every Weight and the Sin Which Doth Easily Beset Us.

A. Anything that would keep us from finishing the race, must be set aside (Heb. 12:1).

B. Many hindered by an improper love (1 John 2:15-17).
C. The Parable of the Sower shows that some will be easily set aside (Matt. 13:19-23).
D. Sin is besetting and will most certainly cause us to lose our reward, if we persist in it and don't repent of it (Luke 13:3; Acts 2:38).
E. We must lay aside our unbelief and believe on the Lord Jesus with all our heart, soul, and mind, or else we will die in our sins (John 8:24).

IV. We Must Run the Race with Patience.

A. The idea here is patient endurance (Heb. 12:1)!
B. Some enter the race through faith and obedience and then don't run the race with patient endurance!
C. We need not expect the prize at the end of the race, if we don't finish!
D. To run with patience is to "run well" (Gal. 5:7).
E. Paul commanded steadfastness (1 Cor. 15:58).
F. Jesus demanded faithfulness (Rev. 2:10).
G. "Blessed is the man that endureth. . ." (Jas. 1:12).

V. We Must Look unto Jesus.

A. Hebrews 12:2
B. Look unto Jesus because He is the author and finisher of our faith.
C. Where else can one look? (John 6:66-68).
D. Jesus is the author of eternal salvation to all those who obey Him (Heb. 5:8-9).
E. He has gone to prepare a place for us (John 14:1-3).

Conclusion

1. The race is set before us, open to all, and brings the greatest reward, Heaven.
2. Won't you enter the race today?

"Men That Hazarded Their Lives"

Introduction

1. Acts 15:22-27
2. The Lord demands that we give our lives entirely unto Him (Mark 8:34-35).
3. Here are some men who hazarded their lives for Christ.

Discussion

I. Barnabas.

A. Acts 15:25-26

B. Barnabas took great measures to help Paul in the gospel (Acts 9:23-31).

C. Barnabas was persecuted for speaking the Word boldly (Acts 13:46-51).

II. Paul.

A. 2 Corinthians 11:23-28

B. Paul put his life in jeopardy for the cause of Jesus Christ (1 Cor. 15:30-32).

C. Paul was willing to die for the Lord (Acts 21:10-13).

III. Silas.

A. Acts 15:26-27

B. Silas was beaten many times and cast into prison for teaching in the name of Christ (Acts 16:19-24).

C. Yet, Silas continued teaching (Acts 17:1-4).

IV. Stephen.

A. Stephen was brought before the council and falsely accused of speaking blasphemy (Acts 6:9-15).

B. Stephen was cast out of the city and stoned to his death (Acts 7:54-60).

V. Peter.

A. Peter and the apostles were threatened by the authorities to not teach in the name of Christ (Acts 5:28-33).

B. Peter and the apostles were beaten (Acts 5:40-42).
C. Peter was imprisoned by Herod because of his stand for the truth (Acts 12:1-6).

VI. John.

A. John was threatened by the authorities to not teach in the Lord's name (Acts 4:13-18).
B. He answered, "We cannot but speak. . ." (Acts 4:20).
C. John was a pillar for the Lord (Gal. 2:9).

VII. Epaphroditus.

A. Philippians 2:25-30
B. Philippians 4:18
C. If you had been Epaphroditus, would you have been described as not regarding your life for the work of Christ?

Conclusion

1. Many of the early disciples hazarded their lives for Christ.
2. We should be willing to do the same.
3. Have you given your life to the Lord?

The Church At Philippi

Introduction

1. One of the finest churches in the New Testament was the church at Philippi.
2. Let me call your attention to some outstanding things about the church at Philippi.

Discussion

I. Had a Scriptural Beginning.

A. Acts 16 finds Paul and company in Philippi.
B. Lydia hears, believes, and is baptized (Acts 16:14-15).
C. The jailor believes and is baptized (Acts 16:23-34).
D. This was the scriptural beginning of the church in the city of Philippi. It came as a result of folks hearing, believing, and obeying the gospel of Christ!

II. Was Fully Organized.

A. Many churches today are not organized after the New Testament pattern.
B. Philippians 1:1

III. Supported Gospel Preaching.

A. Philippians 1:5
B. Philippians 4:16
C. We need more churches that support gospel preachers at home and abroad.

IV. Bold to Speak.

A. Paul was grateful for the boldness of this church.
B. Philippians 1:14
C. We need more boldness among brethren when it comes to teaching the truth!

V. Did Evangelism God's Way.

A. The church sent directly to the needs of Paul in doing their work of evangelism (Phil. 4:15-16).

B. Many churches today are not content with doing evangelism God's way.

VI. Worshipped God.

A. Philippians 3:3
B. God must be worshipped in spirit and in truth (John 4:24).
C. Revelation 22:8-9; Matthew 4:10; Acts 2:42; Ephesians 5:19

VII. Always Obeyed God.

A. Philippians 2:12
B. Even obeyed in Paul's absence!

Conclusion

We need more churches like the church at Philippi!

The Importance of Regular Church Attendance

Introduction

1. Some have not learned the importance of regular church attendance.
2. Let's notice some good, scriptural reasons to attend regularly.

Discussion

I. To Worship God.
   - A. Matthew 4:10
   - B. John 4:23-24
   - C. Glory is to be given to God in the church (Eph. 3:21).
   - D. We worship by:
     1. Singing (Heb. 2:12; Col. 3:16).
     2. Praying (1 Thess. 5:17).
     3. Giving (1 Cor. 16:2).
     4. Observing Lord's Supper (Acts 20:7; 1 Cor. 11:18, 20).
   - E. Need to worship with regularity!

II. To Obey God.
   - A. Assembling is commanded (Heb. 10:25).
   - B. Acts 2:42
   - C. Some commands of God can only be fulfilled as we assemble together (1 Cor. 11:18, 26-29).

III. To Build Up Our Faith.
   - A. As we come together as God's people we receive much encouragement.
   - B. 1 Peter 2:2; 2 Peter 3:18
   - C. It strengthens our faith to worship God and meet with other Christians.
   - D. Romans 1:11-12
   - E. A means of edifying one another (1 Thess. 5:11).

IV. To Encourage Others.

A. Hebrews 10:22-25

B. ". . . Teaching and admonishing one another" (Col. 3:16).

C. Can become a discouragement when folks don't attend as they ought!

V. Because Jesus Is Present.

A. Matthew 18:20

B. If you knew that Jesus would be at a certain place, would you not go?

VI. To Put God and the Church First in Our Lives.

A. Matthew 22:37

B. Matthew 6:33

C. Some are putting everything else above God and the church.

D. J.C. Penny said, "If a man's business requires so much of his time that he cannot attend Sunday morning and evening worship services, and Wednesday night prayer meeting, then that man has more business than God intended him to have."

Conclusion

Hope we've learned the importance of regular church attendance!

“What Doth the Lord Require of Thee?”

Introduction

1. Text: Micah 6:8
2. The question asked by the prophet Micah a long time ago suggests that the Lord requires certain things of His people. Micah goes on to tell us what He requires.
3. This verse may contain the most comprehensive and all-embracing statements in the Old Testament, “What doth the Lord Require of thee?”

Discussion

I. To Do Good.

A. “He hath shewed thee, O man, what is good. . . ,” that is to say, “do good!”
B. The “good” that He requires is the doing of His will.
C. God is “Good” (Matt. 19:16-17).
D. The “good servant” was told well done (Matt. 25:21).
E. Romans 12:2
F. Ephesians 4:29
G. 1 Thessalonians 5:15, 21
H. Some things are said to be “good and acceptable in the sight of God” (1 Tim. 2:3; 5:4).
I. Peter asked, “And who is he that will harm you, if ye be followers of that which is good?” (1 Pet. 3:13).
J. The Bible speaks of “good works” (Tit. 3:8, 14).
K. This, the Lord *requires!*

II. To Do Justly.

A. To do “justly” is to act toward God and man according to the divine standard of righteousness revealed in His law.
B. To do justly is to “judge righteous judgment” (John 7:24).

C. Jesus said, "Judge not, that ye be not judged. . ." (Matt. 7:1-2).
D. We shall all be judged (Heb. 9:27; 2 Cor. 5:10; Eccl. 12:13-14).
E. God's Word is the standard (Rev. 20:11-15).
F. We would do well to remember the proverb: "He who lives in a glass house should not throw stones."
G. This, the Lord *requires!*

III. To Love Mercy.

A. "To love kindness" (ASV).
B. To "love mercy" or "kindness" is to show a compassionate warmheartedness toward man.
C. Luke 6:36; Matthew 5:7
D. To show mercy is to find it! (Matt. 6:14).
E. To forgive and to be forgiven, to show mercy and to receive mercy: these belong together, as Jesus illustrated in the parable of the unmerciful servant (Matt. 18:21-35).
F. This is what the Lord *requires!*

IV. To Walk Humbly with Thy God.

A. To "walk humbly with thy God" is to recognize the absolute holiness and righteousness of God, and to walk in humble and submissive obedience to Him.
B. Christ was humble (Phil. 2:5-7).
C. The arrogant and boastful are constantly warned (1 Cor. 10:12; Gal. 6:3; Jas. 4:6).
D. We must walk (refers to how we live) humbly (Jas. 4:10, 6; 1 Pet. 5:5; Col. 3:12; Luke 18:14).
E. We must remember that God is Creator and we are His creation.
F. This is what the Lord *requires!*

Conclusion

1. Micah 6:6-8
2. Won't you come doing what the Lord *requires!*

When Two Lions Met

Introduction

1. The lion is king of beasts (Judg. 14:18; Prov. 30:30).
2. Imagine two lions locked up in combat. About 2000 years ago, two lions met in a battle to the finish.

Discussion

I. The Two Lions.

A. Satan (1 Pet. 5:8).
   1. From the beginning he has been maiming and killing (Gen. 3:1-6; John 8:44).
   2. He is still very much at work today!

B. Christ (Rev. 5:5).
   1. Genesis 49:8-10
   2. He came to battle with Satan (1 Tim. 1:15).

C. These two lions would meet in combat (Gen. 3:15).

II. The Importance of the Outcome.

A. This contest was planned by God (Eph. 3:11).

B. The salvation of the world hung on the outcome of the battle (Acts 4:12; 2 Tim. 2:10).

C. Both lions knew the importance of the battle.

III. When the Two Lions Met.

A. They met in Bethlehem of Judaea.
   1. The lion of Judah born (Matt. 2:1).
   2. The old lion pounced to destroy the young lion (Matt. 2:16).
   3. The young lion was victorious (Rev. 12:4-6).

B. They met in a wilderness.
   1. The two lions were in a forty day battle (Matt. 4:1-10).
   2. The lion of Judah triumphed (Matt. 4:11).

C. They met during the personal ministry.

1. The character of Jesus was attacked (Luke 7:34).
2. The authority of Jesus was attacked (Matt. 21:23).
3. Jesus won each conflict!

D. They met in the garden of Gethsemane.
1. Jesus was betrayed (Matt. 26:36-57).
2. The lion was condemned to death under false witness (Matt. 27).
3. Christ was victorious through death (Heb. 2:14-15).

E. They met at the resurrection.
1. In the resurrection, Jesus struck the greatest blow against Satan.
2. All claims were proved true (Rom. 1:4).
3. Satan had hopelessly lost!

F. They will meet at the end of time.
1. Christ will strike the final blow against Satan at the end of time.
2. Matthew 25:41
3. Revelation 20:10

Conclusion

1. How thankful we should be that Christ left Heaven and met Satan in battle that we may gain the victory.
2. Still today the battle continues to rage! Christ will help us win the victory (1 Cor. 15:57).
3. Let us fight against Satan with all of our might!

What's Wrong With Denominationalism?

Introduction

1. One radio station ad said, "Go to a church Sunday. It makes no difference where you attend as long as you attend regularly."
2. Not "a" church, but "the" church (Matt. 16:18; Acts 8:1, 3; Matt. 15:13).
3. Notice what's wrong with denominationalism.

Discussion

I. Has a Human Origin.

A. Started by men like Martin Luther (Lutheran church started in 1530).

B. The Lord built but one church (Matt. 16:18; Zech. 1:16; Isa. 2:2-3). The one body is the church (Eph. 4:4; Col. 1:24).

C. How could one church be as good as another when the Bible talks of only one?

II. Follows a Human Creed Book.

A. "Creed" – "I believe."

B. The Bible is complete and all sufficient (2 Tim. 3:16-17; Jude 3, Col. 2:10; 2 Tim. 4:2; 2 Pet. 1:3).

III. Started at the Wrong Time and Place.

A. Started too late to be the New Testament church.

B. Zechariah 1:16; Isaiah 2:2-3

C. Luke 24:46-47 – In Jerusalem in the last days.

D. Acts 2; Hebrews 1:1-2

E. Notice when and where some churches started.

IV. Wears A Human Name.

A. Salvation only in the name of Christ.

1. Acts 4:12; Philippians 2:9

2. Isaiah 56:5; 62:2; 65:15
3. Acts 11:26; 26:28; 1 Pet. 4:16
4. Romans 16:16
5. Colossians 1:18 – Christ to have the preeminence.

B. Colossians 3:17

V. Makes the Lord's Prayer a Mockery.

A. Jesus prayed that we might all be one (John 17:20-21).
B. How can we be one and be divided into hundreds of religious bodies?
C. Psalm 133:1

VI. Makes "Walking by the Same Rule" Impossible.

A. Philippians 3:15-16
B. Denominations are taught to walk by a different rule than that of the Word of God.
C. Most walk by the creed books!

VII. Makes the Teachings of Ephesians 4:1-6 of No Value.

A. Note the seven ones in Ephesians 4.
B. How many is ONE?

VIII. Makes Worship Vain.

A. Matthew 15:9
B. John 4:24
C. Acts 2:42
D. Adds mechanical music to the command to sing (Heb. 2:12; Eph. 5:19).
E. Leaves out the Lord's Supper on the first day of the week (Acts 20:7).
F. Raises funds in ways different from the New Testament church (1 Cor. 16:2).

IX. Perverts the Organization of the Church.

A. Some only have deacons and no elders (Acts 14:23; Phil. 1:1).
B. Some have a one man rule kind of organization, elder (Tit. 1:5).
C. Some have women elders (1 Tim. 3:1).
D. Many have synods, councils, conferences, and conventions to make laws.

X. Blemishes the Bride.

A. Ephesians 5:23-27
B. 2 Corinthians 11:2
C. Teaches the church is not important.
D. Acts 2:47; Ephesians 5:23 – One groom – many brides.

XI. Contradicts Plain Statements.

A. John 14:6 – ". . . the way. . . ."
B. Matthew 7:13-14 – "strait, narrow, few"

XII. Has False Concepts of the Kingdom.

A. They think it is yet to be established.
B. Mark 9:1; Colossians 1:13; Matthew 16:16-19; 1 Corinthians 12:28; 15:23-24; Revelation 1:9
C. Christ is now King of the kingdom (Rev. 17:14).
D. Christ will not come back to earth to set up a kingdom and rule on the earth for 1,000 years (2 Pet. 3:10).
E. John 18:36

XIII. Perverts the Work of the Church.

A. You name it and they do it!
B. The work of the New Testament church was threefold:
   1. Preaching
   2. Benevolence
   3. Edification
C. Work is spiritual (John 18:36).

XIV. Wear Religious Titles.

A. Reverend, Father, Rabbi, etc.
B. Psalm 111:9; Job 32:21-22; Matthew 23:8
C. Just Peter, James, and John in the New Testament.
D. Preacher, minister, and evangelist are not titles but describe the work to be done.

XV. Pentecostal, Charismatic Movement, Apostolic Concept.

A. Acts 2
B. Many suggest tongue speaking and Holy Spirit baptism essential to being saved.

XVI. Promote Social Gospel.

A. Eating and drinking the order of the day (Rom. 14:17; Acts 2:42).
B. 1 Corinthians 11:22
C. Misuse the word "fellowship."

Conclusion

We must reject the false idea of denominationalism and accept the Biblical teaching concerning the Lord's church.

The Husband as God Would Have Him

Introduction

1. Best marriages are between those who know and submit to God's will.
2. Husbands are responsible to make for a happy marriage.
3. The husband as God would have him is. . .

Discussion

I. One Who Leaves Father and Mother.

A. Matthew 19:5

B. While the husband is still a son, the new relationship takes precedence over the former.

C. The husband becomes head of his own family.

D. Some refuse to leave and parents may be at fault.

II. One Who Cleaves To His Wife.

A. Matthew 19:5-6

B. "Cleaves" – cemented, glued together.

C. Husband and wife become one flesh.

D. Selfishness is often a problem in today's marriages.

E. God does the joining (Matt. 19:6).

III. One Who Is the Head of His Wife.

A. Ephesians 5:23

B. Headship carries the idea of leadership in the family.

C. Does not mean that he is a dictator, but that he exercises good for the entire family.

D. Parallel to Christ and God (1 Cor. 11:3).

IV. One Who Dwells with His Wife According to Knowledge.

A. 1 Peter 3:7

B. Knowledge is important in marriage:
   1. Knowledge of God's will.
   2. Knowledge of marriage relationship.
   3. Knowledge of his wife.
C. Important for husbands to have knowledge concerning their wives.
D. Men and women are different and their moods and temperaments are different.

V. One Who Gives Honor to His Wife.

A. 1 Peter 3:7
B. Husbands must respect, esteem, and value their wives.
C. They are to be honored as a weaker vessel and not subjected to physical abuse.
D. Wives are to be honored as an equal spiritual heir (Gal. 3:28).
E. Many husbands are insensitive to their wife's needs, wants, and opinions.

VI. One Who Provides for the Needs of His Wife.

A. There are physical needs that must be provided for (1 Tim. 5:8).
B. There are relationship needs that must be provided for (1 Cor. 7:1-4).

VII. One Who Truly Loves His Wife.

A. Ephesians 5:25-29, 33
B. Husbands are to love their wives as Christ loved the church and gave Himself for it!
C. 1 John 3:18
D. Wives need to know that they are loved! Say, "I love you!"

Conclusion

1. These things make for happy marriages.
2. This is what God expects and demands and anything less will bring much heartache.

Hospitality

Introduction

1. The Shunammite woman is perhaps best remembered for her hospitality toward Elisha (2 Kings 4:8-10). This was hospitality in its purest sense, in that Elisha was a stranger and the Shunammite woman took him in.
2. Let's think some about hospitality.

Discussion

I. Israel Was Called Upon to Be Hospitable.

A. For they were once strangers (Exod. 22:21).

B. They knew what it was like to be a stranger (Exod. 23:9).

C. A stranger was to be loved as one born in thine own house (Lev. 19:10, 33-34; Deut. 10:18-29).

D. God made provisions for the stranger (Deut. 26:12).

II. Inasmuch as We Do It unto Others, We Do It unto the Lord.

A. Matthew 25:34-46

B. "And these shall go away into everlasting punishment: but the righteous into life eternal" (Matt. 25:46).

III. Hospitality Is Not to Be Done for Recompense.

A. Luke 14:12-14

B. "Recompense" means to give compensation to or to repay.

C. The purpose and the motive for doing such is important!

IV. God's People Ought to Be Given to Hospitality.

A. Romans 12:13

B. "Given" means "to pursue, to follow after or press toward."

C. If we, as God's people, don't pursue it, who will?

D. It ought to be a part of us!

E. Phebe was a "succourer of many" including the apostle Paul (Rom. 16:1-2).

V. Hospitality Is a Forgotten Virtue.

A. Hebrews 13:2

B. There was a time when it was a commendable quality found in most people, but now I'm afraid it is as rare as "hen's teeth."

C. "Be not forgetful to entertain strangers" means don't forget to be hospitable!

D. Neglect of the law of hospitality is illustrated in the case of the rich man and Lazarus (Luke 16:19-25).

VI. Hospitality Should Be Done Without Grudging.

A. 1 Peter 4:9-11

B. "Grudging" means without grumbling or murmuring.

C. It you're going to grumble and complain about doing it, you might as well forget it!

D. Hospitality must be rendered with the proper spirit, if it is to be acceptable unto the Lord!

Conclusion

1. We could use a few good "Shunammite women" today, who are not too busy to offer a cup of cold water in His name!
2. Be a lover of hospitality! The rewards will far outweigh the costs.

What the Lord's Supper Says

Introduction

1. Matthew 26:26-29
2. The Lord's supper has a mighty message and says a lot of things. Thus, we take a look.

Discussion

I. The Kingdom Has Been Established.

A. The Lord's supper was to be observed in the kingdom of God (Matt. 26:29; Luke 22:29-30).

B. The church at Corinth observed the Lord's supper (1 Cor. 11:23-34; 10:16).

C. Therefore, the kingdom is the church and has been established.

II. Jesus Died.

A. 1 Corinthians 11:26

B. Jesus died for sinners (Rom. 5:7-8).

C. The fact that Jesus died means that we can have life (1 Thess. 5:10).

III. The New Testament Is Binding.

A. Matthew 26:28

B. Luke 22:20

C. The New Testament became effective when Christ died on the cross (Heb. 9:15-17).

D. The first covenant has vanished away (Heb. 8:7-13).

IV. Man Is Forgetful.

A. 1 Corinthians 11:24-25

B. The Lord's supper is a memorial to remind us of the death of Jesus Christ.

V. We Must Be United.

A. 1 Corinthians 10:16-17

B. 1 Corinthians 12:20

C. The body is the church (Col. 1:24).
D. Unity is a pleasant thing (Ps. 133:1-3).
E. We must endeavor for unity (Eph. 4:3).

VI. There Is a Need for Self-Examination.

A. 1 Corinthians 11:28
B. 2 Corinthians 13:5
C. We need to take inventory of our lives as we partake of the Lord's supper.

VII. Jesus Will Come Again.

A. 1 Corinthians 11:26
B. Christ has promised to come again (John 14:1-3).
C. Christ will come unexpectedly (2 Pet. 3:10).

Conclusion

1. Surely, the Lord's supper says a lot.
2. Let's believe its message.

Laws of Acceptable Prayer

Introduction

1. Prayer is one of the greatest privileges for the child of God. Yet, it may be the most abused privilege.
2. Notice some laws of acceptable prayer:

Discussion

I. Ask.

A. Matthew 7:7
B. James 1:17
C. James 1:6
D. Many do not have because they do not ask!

II. Must Be Righteous.

A. 1 Peter 3:12
B. John 9:31
C. Proverbs 28:9
D. When we allow sin to prevail in our lives, God will not hear (Isa. 59:1-2).

III. Ask According to God's Will.

A. 1 John 5:14-15
B. We may ask for things that are out of harmony with God's will. This is not acceptable.

IV. Ask in Faith.

A. James 1:6-7
B. Hebrews 11:6
C. Asking for rain and only one lady took an umbrella!

V. Ask with a Forgiving Heart.

A. Ephesians 4:32
B. Matthew 6:12-15
C. Matthew 5:23-24

VI. Ask in the Name of Christ.

A. John 14:13-14

B. Colossians 3:17

C. More than just saying the words. We approach God in prayer by the authority of Christ.

VII. Ask with a Thankful Heart.

A. 1 Thessalonians 5:17-18

B. Many are not thankful enough.

Conclusion

1. Prayer is for the Lord's people.
2. Are you one of His?

The Wife as God Would Have Her

Introduction

1. Wives can be a blessing to the home when they are as God would have them.
2. The wife as God would have her is. . .

Discussion

I. One Who Submits to Her Husband.

A. Ephesians 5:22-24
B. "Submit" means "to yield to or arrange under another."
C. Does not imply inferiority.
D. Some women don't want to "stay by their man," they want to be the man!
E. Her submission does not give the husband the right to misuse her submission. He must treat her with dignity, respect, love, and gentleness.

II. One Who Reverences Her Husband.

A. Ephesians 5:33
B. Reverence has to do with respect and honor.
C. Notice the respect that Sarah had for Abraham (1 Pet. 3:6).

III. One Who Is a Keeper at Home.

A. Titus 2:5
B. Keeper is one domesticated, a worker in the home.
C. She is the guide of the house (1 Tim. 5:14) and every wise man buildeth his house (Prov. 14:1).
D. Important work to be done in the home as a keeper.
E. "The hand that rocks the cradle rules the world!"
F. Some believe that such is unfulfilling and trapping.

IV. One Who Renders Due Benevolence to Her Husband.

A. 1 Corinthians 7:3-5

B. "Render" implies a debt to be paid. This debt is due each other and no one else!
C. Such can prevent sexual immorality from entering the relationship (1 Cor. 7:1).
D. This power of the other's body must not be misused!

V. One Who Loves Her Husband.

A. Titus 2:5
B. Love has been called the golden thread that binds our hearts together.
C. This love is tender affection; an unselfish love; one that is ready to serve; a cherishing love.
D. Love is known by the actions it prompts.
E. Notice love's qualities in 1 Corinthians 13:4-7.

Conclusion

1. These are God-given responsibilities!
2. Proverbs 31:1-12, 28

How Saints Walk

Introduction

1. The Christian life is often described as a walk.
2. One of the key words in Ephesians is the word "walk." It suggests our daily manner of life or behavior. Paul told the Ephesian saints to walk as becometh saints (Eph. 5:1-3). They were to. . .

Discussion

I. Walk in Good Works.

A. Ephesians 2:10

B. The Bible has a lot to say about good works (Matt. 5:16; Acts 9:36; 1 Tim. 6:18; 2 Tim. 3:17; Tit. 2:7, 14; 3:8; Heb. 10:24).

C. We see the value of good works to outsiders in 1 Peter 2:12.

D. Are you walking in good works?

II. Walk Worthily.

A. Ephesians 4:1

B. We are to walk worthy of our vocation (or calling).

C. Our calling (or vocation) refers to the gospel by which we are called (2 Thess. 2:14). Our daily walk must be of like value with the gospel by which we have been called.

D. Are you living the type of worthy life that the gospel of Christ demands?

III. Walk Not after the Flesh.

A. Ephesians 4:17

B. They were to walk as becometh saints and walk not as Gentiles walked (Eph. 4:17-24).

C. It takes courage to engage in the Christian walk!

D. Too many Christians have compromised their standards and have begun to walk after the flesh!

E. Notice the works of the flesh (Gal. 5:19-21).

IV. Walk in Love.

A. Ephesians 5:2
B. How does one "walk in love"? It means to live our lives in a disposition of love, loving God and loving our brother in the Lord.
C. Much is said in God's Word about love (1 John 4:7-12, 16, 19-21).
D. Are you walking in love?

V. Walk as Children of Light.

A. Ephesians 5:8
B. They were once walking in "darkness" but now they are "children of light" or children of God (1 John 1:5) and are to so walk!
C. Walking in the light is the basis of fellowship with God and fellow-Christians (1 John 1:6-7).
D. Christ is the light of the world (John 8:12; 9:5).
E. Are you walking as a child of light?

VI. Walk Circumspectly.

A. Ephesians 5:15
B. One of the ways that we walk circumspectly or carefully is by "redeeming the time" (Eph. 5:16).
C. We must make prudent use of every moment.
D. There are many temptations to use time foolishly!
E. We will give account for the use of our time (Rom. 14:12).
F. Are you redeeming the time?

Conclusion

1. How is your walk as compared with how Paul told the Ephesian saints to walk?
2. If you have not been walking this way, we encourage you to make the necessary changes so you can walk so as to please God.
3. There is no better place to walk than in the Lord Jesus Christ!

Saved Like Noah

Introduction

1. 1 Peter 3:20-21
2. This study is a comparison of the salvation of Noah and our salvation from sin.

Discussion

I. Noah Was Saved by the Grace of God.

- A. Genesis 6:8
- B. We too are saved by God's grace.
  1. Ephesians 2:8
  2. Titus 2:11-12
- C. Noah was not saved by grace alone, and neither are we!

II. Noah Was Saved by Faith.

- A. Hebrews 11:7
- B. Faith is included in our salvation.
  1. John 8:24
  2. Mark 16:16
  3. Hebrews 11:6
- C. Salvation is not by faith only (Jas. 2:24-26).

III. Noah Was Saved by Fear.

- A. Hebrews 11:7
- B. Had Noah not feared God as he did, he would not have been moved to prepare the ark.
- C. Respect and reverence for God enters into our salvation.
  1. Ecclesiastes 12:13
  2. Acts 10:35
  3. Philippians 2:12
  4. Hebrews 12:28
- D. Do you fear God, as Noah did?

IV. Noah Was Saved by Obedience.

A. Hebrews 11:7
B. Noah did all that God said do (Gen. 6:22; 7:5).
C. We are saved by obedience.
   1. Matthew 7:21
   2. Luke 6:46
   3. Hebrews 5:8-9
   4. Romans 6:17-18
D. Have you done all that God has commanded?

V. Noah Was Saved by Water.

A. 1 Peter 3:20
B. Water buoyed up the ark and kept it afloat.
C. As Noah was saved by water, we are saved by baptism.
   1. Mark 16:16
   2. Acts 2:38
   3. Acts 22:16
   4. 1 Peter 3:21
D. Have you been baptized?

VI. Noah Was Saved in the Ark.

A. Salvation was placed in Noah's ark (Gen. 7:1, 7, 9, 13, 15-16, 23; 1 Pet. 3:20).
B. Today, salvation is in Christ (2 Tim. 2:10).
C. Baptism puts one into Christ (Gal. 3:27).
D. Just as all those outside the ark perished, all those outside of Christ will be forever lost.

Conclusion

1. All of these principles enter into our salvation.
2. Have you been saved like Noah?

Spiritual Success

Introduction

1. Most people are interested in success and many books have been written on the subject.
2. Joshua 1:6-9 contains seven rules for spiritual success.

Discussion

I. "Be Strong" (1:6).

A. It's important for God's people to be strong.
B. 1 Corinthians 16:13
C. Ephesians 6:10; 1 Corinthians 14:20
D. 2 Timothy 2:1

II. "Be . . . Very Courageous" (1:7).

A. 2 Peter 1:5 – "Virtue" means "courage."
B. Must endure hardness as a good soldier (2 Tim. 2:3).
C. Acts 28:15
D. Daniel was courageous (Dan. 6:7, 10).

III. "Observe to Do According to All the Law" (1:7).

A. Today, Christ has all authority (Matt. 28:19-20).
B. Acts 10:33
C. Acts 20:26-27 – ". . . all the counsel of God"
D. Acts 4:20; 5:29

IV. "Turn Not from the Word of God to the Right Or to the Left" (1:7).

A. Deuteronomy 4:2; Proverbs 30:6
B. Revelation 22:18-19
C. 2 John 9-11
D. Many today are turning away from God's Word.

V. "Meditate Therein Day and Night" (1:8).

A. Discuss idea of meditate.

B. Psalm 1:1; 119:97-99
C. Deuteronomy 6:7-9

VI. "Be Not Afraid" (1:9).

A. Fear keeps many from doing as they ought.
B. Remember one talent man? (Matt. 25:25).
C. Matthew 10:28; Revelation 21:8

VII. "Neither Be Thou Dismayed" (1:9).

A. "Dismayed" means "to become discouraged."
B. Galatians 6:9
C. Isaiah 41:10
D. Song: "Be not dismayed whate'er be tide, God will take care of you."

Conclusion

1. Results: God will be with you (Josh. 1:9). You will have good success and prosper.
2. Must begin this road to success by being obedient to God's Word.

Great Things in the Book of Jonah

Introduction

1. The book of Jonah is a small book but contains many great things.
2. Let's notice some great things in the book of Jonah.

Discussion

I. A Great Refusal.

A. Jonah 1:1-3
B. Jonah's refusal to go to Nineveh.
C. Went in opposite direction to Tarshish, some two thousand miles west.
D. Many today refuse to do God's will for various reasons.
E. Can't get away from God (Jer. 23:24; Ps. 139:7).
F. Refusing to do God's will does not change God's will!

II. A Great Storm.

A. Jonah 1:4
B. Storm even frightened sailors as it was a great tempest (Jon. 1:12).
C. At Jonah's being thrown over, the storm ceased from raging (Jon. 1:15).
D. Good came from this great storm as it taught Jonah a lesson and it caused sailors to fear God.

III. A Great Fish.

A. Jonah 1:17
B. Jesus called it a whale (Matt. 12:40).
C. God had prepared this great fish (Jon. 1:17) as He prepared the gourd, a worm, and the wind.
D. Fish vomited Jonah out on dry land (Jon. 2:1-10).

IV. A Great City.

A. Jonah 3:1-3

B. Nineveh was the capital city of Assyria.
C. It was a great city as it was the residence of the Assyrian kings and was the most influential city of its time.
D. Great city because it made a great change (Jon. 3:4-5).
E. Matthew 12:41

V. A Great Anger.

A. Jonah 4:1
B. Notice what made Jonah angry (Jon. 3:10).
C. Jonah 4:2-3
D. God asked Jonah, ". . . Doest thou well to be angry?" (Jon. 4:4).
E. Jonah had a bad attitude.

VI. A Great God.

A. Entire story shows God's universal love and grace.
B. God was willing to save even a heathen nation like Assyria if they would repent.
C. Jonah 4:10-11
D. Notice the great contrast between Jonah's attitude and God's attitude.
E. 1 Timothy 2:4

Conclusion

1. Jonah is a minor prophet book with major lessons!
2. Have we learned these lessons?

Mother

Introduction

1. One of the sweetest words ever said is the word "Mother."
2. Let's turn our attention to some of the things the Bible has to say about Mother.

Discussion

I. Honour Mother.

A. "Honour" – "to hold in respect, esteem" (AHD).

B. Exodus 20:12; Ephesians 6:1-3

C. This respect was a ground for national permanence with Israel and a ground of our well-being and longevity upon the Earth.

D. Notice the good attitude of Elisha toward his mother and father (1 Kings 19:19-21).

E. Ancient laws pronounced the death penalty upon those who dishonored parents in act or word (Exod. 21:15,17; Lev. 20:9).

F. Notice the *wisdom* of Proverbs (Prov. 30:11, 17).

G. This honor has to do with the honor that is due them for being our parents, irrespective of our parent's personal merits or demerits.

II. Forsake Not the Law of Mother.

A. Proverbs 6:20-24

B. To "forsake" her law is to give it up; renounce it; or abandon it.

C. I've often heard people say, "I remember something my mother use to say."

D. We all can remember the loving and caring words of a mother's wisdom. Don't forsake her laws!

III. A Foolish Son is the Heaviness of Mother.

A. Proverbs 10:1

B. This verse says something about the *influence* of a child over his parent's happiness.

C. Rebellious children give no thought to the pain they may be inflicting upon their parents.
D. Children have it in their power to make bright the evening of their father's and mother's life, or to cloud it with a deep, dark gloom of hopeless misery.

IV. Despise Not Mother When She Is Old.

A. Proverbs 23:22, 25
B. Proverbs 15:20
C. Old age brings infirmities (Eccl. 12:3-5). Don't despise her for these infirmities (the same infirmities may come your way one day!).
D. Children are to repay their parents (1 Tim. 5:4).
E. Some children take advantage of their parents when they are old (Prov. 28:24).

V. Bring Not Mother to Shame.

A. Proverbs 29:15
B. Mothers have a role here! Often times mothers leave their children, failing to provide the care, love, and guidance they need most.
C. A child left to do as he likes, undisciplined-spoiled, as we call it, is a shame to his mother.
D. Timothy didn't bring his mother to shame (1 Tim. 1:5).
E. Many a mother has been brought to shame by a rebellious and unruly child. Can you begin to imagine the shame and disgrace that a godly mother might bare and take to her grave with her?

Conclusion

1. We need more godly mothers who are instilling God's Word in the hearts of their children.
2. Don't forget to honor your mother (Eph. 6:2).

"Then Cometh The End"

Introduction

1. 1 Corinthians 15:24
2. We take a look at what will happen at the end of time.

Discussion

I. Christ Will Come.

A. John 14:1-3
B. Hebrews 9:28
C. Revelation 22:20
D. The time of His coming is unknown to man (Mark 13:32).
E. We shall meet the Lord in the air (1 Thess. 4:16-17).

II. The Dead Will Be Raised.

A. Death is not the end of things (Eccl. 12:7).
B. There will be a resurrection.
   1. John 5:28-29
   2. John 11:24
   3. Acts 24:15
C. The new body to be resurrected is not described in the Word of God (1 Cor. 15:35-38).

III. The Living Will Be Changed.

A. 1 Corinthians 15:51-52
B. Philippians 3:20-21
C. The reason we will be changed is flesh and blood cannot inherit the kingdom of God (1 Cor. 15:50).
D. Our bodies are corruptible, subject to death and decay, but the spiritual body will be incorruptible.

IV. The Present World Will End.

A. The earth is only temporary.

B. 2 Peter 3:10-11
C. 1 John 2:17
D. We await a new dwelling place (2 Pet. 3:13).
E. Have you made your reservations for Heaven?

V. All Will Be Judged.

A. Ecclesiastes 12:13-14
B. 2 Corinthians 5:10
C. Revelation 20:12
D. Jesus will be the judge (John 5:22; Acts 17:30-31)
E. The judgment will be just (2 Tim. 4:8; John 5:30).
F. The Word of God will be the standard of judgment (John 12:48; Rom. 2:16; Rev. 20:12).

VI. The Kingdom Will Be Delivered Up.

A. 1 Corinthians 15:24
B. The kingdom is the church (Matt. 16:18-19).
C. The Lord's kingdom is not of this world (John 18:36). It is a spiritual kingdom (Phil. 3:20).
D. Are you in the kingdom?

VII. The Reign of Christ Will End.

A. Christ is reigning now on the heavenly throne and will reign until the end comes (1 Cor. 15:24-28).
B. Christ was given dominion, glory, and a kingdom when He ascended to God (Dan. 7:13-14; Eph. 1:19-23).
C. He will reign till there are no more dead.

Conclusion

1. We do not know when the end will come.
2. Are you ready for that day to come?

www.ingramcontent.com/pod-product-compliance
Lightning Source LLC
LaVergne TN
LVHW090935080826
845145LV00003B/762

* 9 7 8 1 5 8 4 2 7 3 3 5 6 *